HUNTER DAVIES'

BOOK OF

LISTS

An Intriguing Collection of Facts & Figures

Researcher: Caitlin Davies

THUNDER'S MOUTH PRESS
NEW YORK

HUNTER DAVIES' BOOK OF LISTS
AN INTRIGUING COLLECTION OF FACTS AND FIGURES

Published by
Thunder's Mouth Press
An Imprint of Avalon Publishing Group Inc.
245 West 17th St., 11th Floor
New York, NY 10011

AVALON
publishing group incorporated

First published in Great Britain in 2004 by Cassell Illustrated

First Thunder's Mouth Press printing October 2005

Library of Congress PCN Number: 2005929431

ISBN 1-56025-785-7

9 8 7 6 5 4 3 2 1

Printed in China
Distributed by Publishers Group West

CONTENTS

~

Introduction

As we stagger through life, we all make lists. It's one of the signs of human behavior—as soon as they had crawled out of their caves, humans were compiling lists of animals hunted and their favorite words.

Lists, roughly speaking, come in three types. Some are mental props written either on scraps of paper or in our heads, listing jobs to be done, objects to be acquired, actions to be taken. These are functional lists, serving a specific purpose. Then there are factual lists, detailing globules of information that don't necessarily require any action to be taken: facts roughly connected and set out in an order, or just all the facts gathered on the same subject, in no particular order. Then there are lists that are just opinions: my favorite desserts, my best Beatles' singles, my top films, my worst holiday, people I really really like.

If those are the three basic types of list, we then come to an interesting subdivision: male lists and female lists. Women, on the whole, are mainly concerned with lists as mental aids, listing vital things to be done, presents to be bought, meals to be cooked. They have so many things to remember that out of necessity rather than whimsy they create lists. The very process of writing the list seems to help clear their minds. Often, they will make a list after they have done all the chores—writing out the list, then ticking off things already done, feeling really pleased, even though nobody knows. Strange.

The second type of list, factual, tends to be a mainly male preserve. Sports records are the obvious example, or all their CDs, in alphabetical order. Is it because men are trying to gain control over their life—or trying to escape it? Or are they simply geeks?

The third type of list, based on opinions, is again almost wholly male: England's best-ever strikers or their favorite childhood TV shows. I was in the kitchen of a young couple recently, and their bulletin board had two lists—one listed flour, something for nits, tights, birthday card, gas board. The other listed Owen, Rooney, Beckham, Campbell, anyone but Gary Neville. Each list was ongoing, being deleted and added to every day, destined forever to go their separate ways.

I've always loved lists, of any sort, trivial or otherwise. My oldest surviving list, made as an adult, now kept in the pages of our family

Bible, was when our first child was about to be born and I was listing possible names–Caitlin, Morag, Kirsten, Amanda, Lucy or Mark, Gavin, Simon, Callum, Saul, Adam. They reflect the popular names back in the sixties. My wife looks at the list now and says, "Impossible, I could never have wanted the name Morag, that must have been you."

In 1980 I published a book called *The British Book of Lists*. It was partly a pinch from a similar American book, which contained just American lists, but also a way of clearing out and using up all the daft lists and odd facts I had accumulated over the years. I also thought of new lists and hired people short of a few pennies to call firms such as Marks & Spencer to find out what their best-selling items were the previous week (chicken first, then ladies' sweaters). I also asked my neighbor, the late A. J. P. Taylor, to make a list of prime ministers who had been adulterers. Little did I know this list would ever be added to. The book was a big success and for the next few years came out in many reprints and new editions, including a children's version for charity.

Twenty-five years later, the world is awash with lists. Government and official departments are obsessed with churning out the latest figures to show how well they are doing; the Internet is loaded with lists, many of them unreliable, not to say dodgy. On TV, radio, newspapers, magazines, and from corporate bodies all over the globe, endless lists are being turned out, but disguised as news, surveys, research, and opinion polls.

This modest little offering is meant as light reading, a stocking-filler, an amusement while traveling. I am grateful to my daughter Caitlin, who as a little girl helped on the first edition and is now an author in her own right, for doing most of the real hard work.

The lists are different, because the world is different and our interests have changed. We have steered away from many of the factual types of lists we created last time, which are now commonplace, done by everyone, so, alas, no more Marks & Spencer chicken . . .

—HUNTER DAVIES
LONDON, JUNE 2004

Some damning reviews
and comments

Classic songs
and their origins

Some modern
classic songs
and their origins

TV footage

Most complained-about
advertisements

Great *Guardian* corrections

Most stolen artists

THE
ARTS
AND
MEDIA

Some damning reviews and comments

On authors, composers, and artists who went on,
surprisingly, to be pretty well thought of nonetheless
by posterity.

AUTHORS

J. M. Barrie: "Oh, for an hour of Herod." Novelist Anthony Hope, after the first night of *Peter Pan*.

A. A. Milne: "I see no future for Mr. A. A. Milne, whose plots are as thin as a filleted anchovy." Critic H. Dennis Bradley, 1925.

Samuel Beckett: "I've been brooding in my bath and it is my considered opinion that *Waiting for Godot* is the end of theater as we know it." Actor Robert Morley.

Lord Byron: "We counsel him to forthwith abandon poetry." *Edinburgh Review*.

William Wordsworth: "This, we think, has the merit of being the very worst poem we ever saw printed in a quarto volume." Lord Jeffrey in the *Edinburgh Review* on Wordsworth's "The White Doe of Rylstone," 1815.

Joseph Conrad: "I cannot abide Conrad's souvenir-shop style, bottled ships and shell necklaces of romantic clichés." Russian novelist Vladimir Nabokov.

D. H. Lawrence: "Filth. Nothing but obscenities." Joseph Conrad.

Charles Dickens: "It would take a heart of stone not to laugh aloud at the death of Little Nell." Oscar Wilde.

Thomas Hardy: "When I finished the story I opened the windows and let the fresh air in." American critic, anon., on *Jude the Oscure*.

Henry James: "An idiot, and a Boston idiot to boot, than which there is nothing lower in the world." Writer H. L. Mencken.

James Joyce: "James Joyce is rather inaudible because he is talking to himself." G. K. Chesterton.

Jack Kerouac: "That's not writing, that's typing." Truman Capote.

Norman Mailer: "It's a fake. A clever, talented, admirably executed fake." Gore Vidal on *The Naked and the Dead*.

Abraham Lincoln: "The president acted without sense, so let us pass over his silly remarks." *The Patriot*, Harrisburg, on Lincoln's Gettysburg Address.

COMPOSERS

Beethoven: "Beethoven always sounds to me like the upsetting of bags of nails." John Ruskin.

Berlioz: "This is the way Berlioz composes—he splutters the ink over the pages of ruled paper and the result is as chance wills it." Frédéric Chopin.

Chopin: "The entire works of Chopin present a motley surface of ranting hyperbole and excruciating cacophony." *Musical World*, 1841.

Haydn: "A mere fop . . . a scribbler of songs." Gregorious Werner, contemporary composer.

Gustav Mahler: "A detailed annotation of what the music would be like if only the composer could think of the right notes." *Musical Times*, 1931, on Mahler's Symphony No. 2.

Puccini: "The opera has been produced with great success in . . . Italy and South America . . . and as far as I am concerned, the places are welcome to it." *Morning Post*, 1906, on *Tosca*.

Schubert: "Perhaps a more overrated man never existed." *Musical Times*, 1897.

Tchaikovsky: "His first piano concerto, like the first pancake, is a flop." Russian critic Nicolai Soloviev.

Richard Wagner: "Wagner has good moments, but bad quarter-hours." Gioacchino Rossini.

ARTISTS

Degas: "Degas is nothing but a peeping tom." *The Churchman*, May 1886.

Jacob Epstein: "Stone carving doesn't happen to be what he's best at." Fellow sculptor Eric Gill.

Henry Moore: "The statues are hideous beyond words." *Morning Post*, 1929.

Paul Gaugin: "All of his figures have a smutty look." John Burroughs.

Monet: "It is only too easy to catch people's attention by doing something worse than anyone has dared to do it before." Anon. reviewer in *Charivari*.

J. M. W. Turner: "This brown thing–is this your Turner?" Monet.

Augustus John: "The latest paintings are worthless. There is less talent than trick." Art critic Clive Bell, *New Statesman*, June 1938.

Whistler: "I have heard much of cockney impudence before now, but never expected to hear a coxcomb ask 200 guineas for flinging a pot of paint in the public's face." John Ruskin.

Picasso: "If I met Picasso in the street, I would kick him in the pants." Sir Alfred Munnings, President of the Royal Academy.

Graham Sutherland: "It makes me look half-witted, which I ain't." Winston Churchill, on his portrait by Sutherland.

Classic songs and their origins

SUMMER IS ICUMEN IN, 1240: Thought to be our oldest existing popular song. Written by John of Fornsette, a monk at Reading, on hearing the first cuckoo of the year.

GREENSLEEVES, c.1540: Mentioned by Shakespeare in *The Merry Wives of Windsor*. Allegedly composed by Henry VIII.

GOLDEN SLUMBERS, c.1600: Original words by Thomas Dekker. Paul McCartney had fun with the words on "Abbey Road," but used his own tune.

POP GOES THE WEASEL, 1620: Created by the pilgrim fathers as a singing game, later adopted by London hatters. In 1961 Anthony Newley turned it into a Top 20 hit.

THE FIRESHIP, c.1650: A sea shanty that became "The Rakish Kind" and then a 1951 hit for Guy Mitchell as "The Roving Kind."

BARBARA ALLEN, 1666, which was when Samuel Pepys mentioned it in his diary, so it's presumably even older.

I GAVE MY LOVE A CHERRY, 1680: Also known as "The Riddle Song." Melody later used by Donny Osmond for "The Twelfth of Never."

HARK THE HERALD ANGELS SING, 1739: Words written by Charles Wesley, but since lifted onto millions of Christmas cards.

GOD SAVE THE QUEEN, or KING, as the case may be, 1745: Written as a battle cry for the House of Hanover. Words by Henry Carey. The more triumphalist verses have now been quietly dropped.

GOD REST YOU MERRY GENTLEMEN, 1770: Interesting from a punctuation point of view–was originally: "God rest you merry, gentlemen," but the comma and the original sense got lost.

AULD LANG SYNE, 1789, which was when Robert Burns added the words, but the tune dates back to 1687. Sung throughout the civilized world on New Year's Eve–especially Millennium eve.

SILENT NIGHT, 1818: A young Austrian priest, Joseph Mohr, wrote the words after visiting a woodcutter's wife who had just given birth. The village organist added a tune.

ABIDE WITH ME, 1847: One Sunday, the Reverend Henry Francis Lyte preached a sermon, wrote this hymn–and then died.

WAY DOWN UPON THE SWANNEE RIVER, 1852: Written by Stephen Foster. He had never seen the Swannee–just liked the name.

JINGLE BELLS, 1857: Written by a Boston teacher, James Pierpont, for a Sunday school Christmas show.

D'YE KEN JOHN PEEL, 1869, which was when William Metcalfe, choirmaster at Carlisle Cathedral, wrote the tune we now know. The words were written in 1829 by John Woodcock Graves in honor of his friend John Peel, a famous Caldbeck huntsman. Now sung by huntsmen, and Cumbrians, everywhere.

SWING LOW, SWEET CHARIOT, 1872: Written by Sarah Sheppard after being talked out of suicide. Originally "Swing Down, Sweet Chariot." African slave workers had visions of chariots sweeping down to take them to heaven. Now England's adopted rugby song.

HAPPY BIRTHDAY TO YOU, 1893: The song was actually composed, not taken out of the air, by two American sisters and nursery teachers, Mildred and Patty Hill. Originally "Good Morning to You." Later changed to "Happy Birthday." Used by Western Union in the thirties as a singing telegram, until they were sued for breach of copyright.

Source: Brother, Can You Spare a Dime?, *Spencer Leigh, 2000*

Some modern classic songs and their origins

YOU'LL NEVER WALK ALONE, 1945: Written by Rodgers and Hammerstein for their musical *Carousel*. Frank Sinatra and Judy Garland did quite well with it at the time, but it was Gerry and the Pacemakers' version in 1963 that turned it into Liverpool's, and then soccer's, anthem.

ROCK AROUND THE CLOCK, 1955: Bill Haley and the Comets. Haley was thirty at the time, but looked older, plump, and decidedly unsexy, with a silly *coif*. It was the song's inclusion in the teen film *Blackboard Jungle*, causing kids in the U.S. and UK to dance in the aisles and tear up seats, which made it a worldwide hit. Now seen as arguably the first rock'n'roll record.

MY WAY, 1967: English words written by Paul Anka to an existing French tune. Frank Sinatra first recorded it in 1969–and it became his anthem, although he later came to dislike it.

CANDLE IN THE WIND, 1974: Elton John with words by Bernie Taupin. Song was originally a tribute to Marilyn Monroe, addressing her by her real name, Norma Jean, but the words were altered in 1997 in memory of Diana, Princess of Wales, and performed at her funeral in Westminster Abbey by Elton John.

LOVE IS ALL AROUND, 1967: A minor period hit for that very 1960s group the Troggs. Reg Presley said he knocked it out in fifteen minutes. Didn't really become a smash hit until it was used in *Four Weddings and a Funeral* in 1994.

NO WOMAN, NO CRY, 1975: Recorded live by Bob Marley and the Wailers at the Lyceum in London. Written by Marley, remembering his life in Trenchtown, Jamaica. Helped make him the first reggae singer to become a world superstar.

THRILLER, 1983: Michael Jackson. The title of his album, which became the best-selling album of all time, with 35 million copies sold. Helped along by a 14-minute dance video, which generated more interest than the song itself.

EVERY BREATH YOU TAKE, 1983: Sting. Written by him in Jamaica, while staying at Goldeneye, Ian Fleming's old house. Unable to sleep, he got up in the night and wrote it.

YESTERDAY, 1965: The Beatles. Paul McCartney says the song came to him in a dream. When he woke up, he wrote it down as "Scrambled eggs, oh my baby how I love your legs," but decided those words were too silly to go with a beautiful tune. "Yesterday" is now the most covered popular song of all time—over 3,000 versions had been recorded at the last count.

TV footage

Footage of the September 11, 2001 attacks on New York is shown more often on television than any other recent news event. But pictures of Neil Armstrong's 1969 walk on the moon are still the most requested archive footage at ITN, whose newsreels date back to 1896. In an article published in the *Independent*, Alwyn Lindsey, managing director of their archives, said that the the key to memorable television moments is a combination of visual impact and historical significance. He believes footage of September 11 will overtake Armstrong on the moon as the most requested archive footage ever.

Most requested archive footage (ITN, Reuters, Channel Four, British Pathe)
1. Neil Armstrong's moonwalk, 1969
2. The assassination of John F. Kennedy, 1963
3. The funeral of Diana, Princess of Wales, 1997
4. Bobby Moore lifting the World Cup, 1966
5. The SAS storming of the Iranian embassy in London, 1980
6. Margaret Thatcher's tearful departure from 10 Downing Street, 1990
7. Neville Chamberlain's "Peace for our time" speech, 1938
8. Hindenburg disaster, 1937
9. Atomic blasts at Hiroshima and Nagasaki, 1945

Most complained-about advertisements

Every year in the UK hundreds of people contact the Advertising Standards Authority (ASA) to complain about an advertisement that has offended or upset them. Yet one of the most complained-about ads in 2003 was also voted one of the best in the industry.

An advertising campaign by Barnardo's, the children's charity, was banned by the ASA for its use of "shocking images." One ad showed a huge, computer-generated cockroach emerging from the mouth of a newborn baby. Barnardo's said the ads "caused distress for good reason," just like road safety advertisements. But 466 people registered a complaint and the ASA ruled that the campaign could "cause serious or widespread offense."

Shortly afterwards, *Campaign* magazine voted the Barnardo's campaign number six in its Top 10 for 2003.

SOME OF THE MOST COMPLAINED-ABOUT
ADVERTISEMENTS BETWEEN 1995–2003

1. British Safety Council advertisement aimed at raising awareness for National Condom Week, 1995. A leaflet featuring Pope John Paul II wearing a safety helmet above the text: "Thou shalt always wear a condom."
   1,187 complaints, which were upheld.

2. Yves Saint Laurent poster for a perfume, showing a naked woman lying on her back, 2000. Complainants said the image was degrading to women, the advertisers said it was a "work of art."
   948 complaints, which were upheld.

3. A. G. Barr poster advertising Irn Bru, 1998. The poster featured a cow next to the text: "When I'm a burger, I want to be washed down with Irn Bru."
   589 complaints, not upheld.

4. Club 18–30 (a UK travel agency) series of advertisements, 1995. The posters and press advertisements featured headlines such as: "You get two weeks for being drunk and disorderly," "It's not all sex, sex, sex. There's a bit of sun and sea as well," and "Girls, can we interest you in a package holiday?" above a photograph of a man with a prominent bulge in his boxer shorts. Complainants said the posters were obscene, irresponsible, and offensive. The advertisers said they reflected the essence of the holidays through humor and colloquialisms.
   490 complaints, which were upheld.

5. Gossard poster for underwear, 1996. The posters were headed: "Who said a woman can't get pleasure from something soft" next to a woman in her underwear lying on the grass.
   321 complaints, not upheld.

Great *Guardian* corrections

UK newspaper the *Guardian* used to be well known for typographical mistakes, much to the amusement of all other papers. My favorite is from September 11, 1986, on the Sports pages about a Scotland soccer game. I still have it pinned on my wall:

> "One day the great manager and the great team will arrive and the blue shits will assume their rightful place on top of the world."

Since then, modern technology has greatly reduced such printing errors, but the *Guardian* now makes a great virtue of each week correcting any factual, grammatical, or stylistic mistakes their writers may make.

On January 3, 2004, looking back at the previous year, they printed a selection of that year's more interesting corrections and clarifications:

> Interview with Sir Jack Hayward, chair of Wolverhampton Wanderers: "Our team was the worst in the First Division and I'm sure it'll be the worst in the Premier League."
>
> Sir Jack had just declined the offer of a hot drink, and what he actually said was: "Our tea was the worst in the First Division and I'm sure it'll be the worst in the Premier League."

> St. Andrews University does not sport an apostrophe, and nor does the town of the same name.

> A picture of the queen was flipped, making her appear to be left-handed.

> A report about nineteenth-century Lowther Castle said Boswell, Hogarth, and Pitt had visited. Boswell died in

1795, Hogarth in 1764, Pitt the Elder in 1778, and Pitt the Younger in 1806.

In an article on health and clothing, the optimum temperature of testicles was given as 22 degrees Celsius below core body temperature (instead of 2.2 degrees).

Most stolen artists

Stealing a famous painting by a famous artist seems a pretty silly thing to do. For a start, how can you sell it? Even if you put it on your own wall, someone might recognize it. But there have always been unprincipled millionaires, with very secure walls in very secure, well-hidden mansions, willing to ogle their favorite artist in total privacy. And, of course, there's the insurance. Having stolen the painting, keep it hidden for a while, then do a secret deal with the insurance firms.

In recent years, another reason has emerged for swiping a masterpiece–keeping it as a Get out of Jail Free Card. The Art and Artists Unit of the Metropolitan Police now believe that many professional thieves steal famous works of art and stash them away, then when they get caught for some other crime say, "Psst, wanna know where a twenty-million-dollar Picasso is hidden?" They then attempt to decrease their sentence by supplying the information.

Whatever the reasons, stealing masterpieces is on the increase. The Art Loss Register, a London-based company, holds records of 140,000 paintings stolen from all around the world. And they have kindly revealed the Top 10 most popular artists considered worth running away with . . .

Top 10	Artist	Number of works stolen
1.	Pablo Picasso	551
2.	Joan Miró	356
3.	Marc Chagall	309
4.	Salvador Dalí	231
5.	Pierre-Auguste Renoir	209
6.	Albrecht Dürer	203
7.	Rembrandt van Rijn	174
8.	Andy Warhol	159
9.	David Teniers	127
10.	Henri Matisse	108

Source: Art Loss Register

Starting young

First jobs of the famous

Backstage demands

Starting old

**Burial places of
the famous**

CELEBRITIES

Starting young

Here's a list of some interesting and also some awful events that happened to people when they were very, very young.

Age 1: Charles Lindbergh III, son of the famous American aviator Colonel Lindbergh, was kidnapped. A ransom was paid, but the baby was later found dead.

Age 2: Princess Anne began riding lessons. They were not wasted, for she later rode for Britain in the Olympics and in 1971 was voted BBC Sportswoman of the Year.

Age 3: Elizabeth Taylor gave her first Royal Command Performance–dancing with her ballet class before the king and queen in 1935.

Age 4: Malcolm X, the African American activist leader, saw his family home burned down by the Ku Klux Klan.

Age 5: The Dalai Lama was enthroned as spiritual and temporal leader of Tibet, in 1940. He was later forced to flee by Chinese Communists.

Age 6: Wolfgang Amadeus Mozart was writing minuets and touring the courts of Europe, giving recitals on the violin.

Age 7: Thomas Macaulay, British historian, who had learned to read at age three, started compiling a history of the world.

Age 8: Charlie Chaplin appeared on stage in a clog-dancing routine called "Eight Lancashire Lads."

Age 9: Lord Byron was supposedly introduced to sex by his family nurse, an otherwise devout Scottish girl, who crept into his bed and "aroused him sexually." She also allowed him to watch her making love.

Age 10: Louis XVII of France died. His father, Louis XVI, and mother were guillotined during the French Revolution. The surviving French nobles declared young Louis the next king, but at age eight he was imprisoned and died two years later.

First jobs of the famous

Or at least jobs they had in their early years, before they became famous for what they became famous for. In show business it's pretty normal to have a variety of jobs before making it, but it can also happen in other professions and careers.

Warren Beatty–rat catcher
Bruce Willis–truck driver
Michael Douglas–gas station attendant
Michael Caine–meat market porter
Steve McQueen–towel boy in brothel
Jack Nicholson–mailroom boy at MGM
Glenda Jackson–shop assistant at a pharmacy
Raquel Welch–secretary to a bishop
Sean Connery–milkman
Sylvester Stallone–beautician
Roger Moore–male model for knitting patterns
Marilyn Monroe–aircraft factory worker
Jeremy Irons–street musician
Tom Cruise–gardener
Bob Hoskins–sailor in Norwegian merchant navy
Mick Jagger–porter in a mental hospital
Sting–clerk in Inland Revenue
Annie Lennox–fish factory worker
Cilla Black–hairdresser
Ozzy Osbourne–slaughterhouse laborer

Elton John–messenger boy for music publisher
Kylie Minogue–shop assistant
Paul McCartney–electrical coil winder
Tom Jones–apprentice glove cutter
Julio Iglesias–goalkeeper at Real Madrid (youth soccer team)
Dame Kiri te Kanawa–telephone operator
Dame Shirley Bassey–chamberpot factory worker
Rod Stewart–grave digger
Phil Collins–painter and decorator
Madonna–waitress at burger bar
Jasper Carrott–traveling denture paste salesman
Dawn French–teacher
Billy Connolly–welder
Julie Walters–nurse
David Jason–garage mechanic

Abraham Lincoln–postman
George Bush Sr.–equipment clerk
John Major–construction worker
Ken Livingstone–lab technician
Hitler–designer of advertising posters for deodorants
Mussolini–chocolate factory worker
Alexander Fleming–shipping clerk
Pope John Paul II–quarry laborer
Tchaikovsky–office clerk
Gaugin–stockbroker's agent
Van Gogh–schoolteacher
Charles Dickens–shoe polish factory worker
Mark Twain–apprentice printer
Robert Louis Stevenson–lawyer
Somerset Maugham–doctor
Thomas Hardy–architect
Walt Disney–apple masher in jelly factory
Diana, Princess of Wales–children's nanny
Socrates–stone worker

Backstage demands

Music stars often have very specific requirements for their dressing rooms–as outlined in their contracts. They cover obvious professional requirements such as stage design, sound systems, and lighting, but very often include the artist's own personal demands.

U2 Zoo TV Tour, 1992
1 case Rolling Rock or a local domestic bottled beer
4 cases Heineken
½ case Guinness Stout
1 x 5th Cuervo Tequila
1 x 5th Stolli or Absolut Vodka
1 x 5th Jack Daniel's Black
2 x 5ths Moet White Star Champagne
3 very good French white Chardonnay
3 very good French red Bordeaux
2 Mouton Cadet red wines
2 Jacobs Creek or Black Opal Australian white wine
1 medium-quality Port or Sherry

**Sting's dressing room, 2000 Tour,
North American leg**
6 large bath-size towels and two bars of soap
Carpeting
Low-key lighting
2-seater couch
2 armchairs
A table for catering requirements
2 coffee tables
2 large bottles Evian Water (on ice)
2 large bottles Evian Water (room temperature)
1 bottle full-bodied red wine
Hot tea
Kettle
Teapot

Cups
Saucers
12 fresh lemons
1 jar of honey
Fresh, skinned and grated ginger root

Backstreet Boys catering requirements
All meals must be prepared in-house.
No take-out meals or fast food will be accepted.
All meals are to be sit-down meals with clean tablecloths,
    real plates (no paper), silverware, real coffee cups.

Deli tray and bread:
Available throughout the day
Sandwich meat
Cheese
Crackers and chips
Butter, mustard, mayo, etc.
Assorted breads
A bowl of fruit

Large bowl of soup:
To be out at 3:30 each day for the arrival of the artist

Breakfast:
To be served at a time determined by at load in
Eggs
Bacon
Sausage
Assortment of cold cereal
Assorted breads
Jelly
Peanut butter
Fresh fruit
Yogurt in assorted flavors

Lunch:
To be served around 12:00 noon
Hot sandwiches
Hamburgers
French dip
Hot turkey
Sloppy Joes
Tacos
2 types of salad
1 type of soup
Condiments as needed

Dinner:
To be served no less than two hours before BSB on stage
1 chicken dish
1 beef dish
1 vegetarian or fish dish
2 side dishes
Cooked vegetables
Potatoes
Rice
Beans

P. Diddy catering requirements
1. A catering representative must be present at all times.
2. Before serving, all food and ice must be inspected for hair, package, paper, etc. and all catering staff must wear hair nets.
3. All drinks should be iced down 20 minutes prior to serving in large trash containers lined with plastic bags.
4. Total number of towels needed for day of the show:
   nine dozen bath-size towels (Crew)
   eight dozen hand-size towels (Artist)
   twenty bars of soap for showers

5. Please try to avoid the frying of food in daily meals unless it is necessary and include low-fat cooking products and condiments.
6. All juices in dressing rooms should be in boxes unless otherwise specified.

Luciano Pavarotti miscellaneous requirements
There must be no distinct smells anywhere near the Artist.
There cannot be any flowers located backstage in the dressing room, or around the stage.
There is to be no smoking backstage, nor is there to be any noise.

Kenny G's dressing room requirements
Large, clean floor carpet
Nice fresh flower arrangement with Japanese flair
2 x 8 foot tables with tablecloths and skirts
2 lamps
2 chairs
Closet or clothes rack with hangers
AC outlets
Mirror
Soap
12 towels
Shower and lavatory facilities with access to only Kenny G

Kenny G's chef's room:
Running hot and cold water
2 x 8 foot tables
3 bath tubs
4 x 110w outlets
12 complete meal flatware setups
Silverwear

No plastic
No styrofoam
12 x 8-ounce glasses
Cloth napkins
4 quart chafing dish with sterno and serving utensils
1 whisk
Mixing bowl

Source: www.thesmokinggun.com

Starting old

Here's a list of some startling achievements by people during their supposed later and declining years.

Age 70: Alfred Wallis, Cornish primitive artist, first started to paint. Until then he had been a cabin boy, fisherman, and rag-and-bone man, until he retired. When his wife died, he started to paint marine scenes. Artist Ben Nicholson saw them and made Wallis's work known worldwide.

Age 71: Leni Riefenstal, Hitler's favorite documentary filmmaker, took up scuba diving, lying about her age and saying she was only 51.

Age 72: The Marquis de Sade acquired his last mistress. He persuaded her to shave off her pubic hair for him. He died two years later, in 1841.

Age 73: Konrad Adenauer became chancellor of Germany, in 1949, remaining in office until 1963.

Age 76: John XXII became pope in 1958, but lasted only five years.

Age 77: Clara Barton, founder of the American Red Cross, went off to serve in Cuba during the Spanish-American War of 1898.

Age 78: Sir Thomas Beecham, the conductor, set off on an international tour with the Royal Philharmonic Orchestra.

Age 79: Dame Edith Evans, English actress, won the New York Critics Award in 1967 for her performance in *The Whisperers*.

Age 80: George Burns, American comedian, won an Oscar for *The Sunshine Boys* in 1976, becoming the oldest person to win an Oscar.

Age 81: Benjamin Franklin, statesman and scientist, helped to frame the U.S. Constitution in 1787.

Age 82: Winston Churchill published the first part of his four-volume work, *A History of the English-Speaking Peoples*.

Age 82: Bill Kane, the American cowboy, was still riding rodeo at the age of 82. His secret was never to miss his daily workout.

Age 83: Agatha Christie celebrated in 1974 the fact that her play *The Mousetrap*, which had opened in 1952, had established the record for the world's longest-running play in the same theater. Even then it didn't close, but moved down the road to another theater.

Age 84: Claude Monet completed one of his greatest works, a series of murals for the orangery beside his water lily pond at Giverny, France.

Age 85: Coco Chanel, still running her fashion empire, had a musical based on her life open on Broadway, with Katharine Hepburn in the leading role.

Age 86: Elizabeth Blackwell, the first woman to qualify as a doctor in the U.S., was in 1907 still practicing as a gynecologist.

Age 87: Bernard Berenson, American art critic and collector, completed the third part of his autobiography.

Age 87: George Burns, the American comedian, gave a special performance for the queen when he was 87.

Age 88: Pablo Casals, the great Spanish cellist, continued to give concerts around the world.

Age 89: Albert Schweitzer, French missionary doctor, was still in charge of the hospital he had established in Gabon, West Africa.

Age 89: Mary Baker Eddy was still in control of the Church of Christ Scientist (the Christian Scientist movement) at 89, an organization which she founded.

Age 90: Margaret Murray, British archaeologist, became president of the English Folklore Society. She was writing books until she was 100.

Age 91: Eamon de Valera was still president of the Irish Republic, but retired the same year and died two years later.

Age 92: Fenner Brockway, Labour MP and peace campaigner, published his book *Britain's First Socialists*.

Age 93: William Dubois, American historian and leading figure in the National Association for the Advancement of Colored People, converted to communism.

Age 94: Bertrand Russell, English philosopher, was still active as an antiwar and nuclear arms campaigner.

Age 95: Arthur Rubenstein, pianist, gave his last public concert, the oldest-known age for any virtuoso concert performer.

Age 96: Grandma Moses, already enormously successful in the U.S., gave her first exhibition of paintings in London.

Age 97: Winifred Rushforth, Scottish doctor and psychoanalyst, was still conducting dream therapy groups in Edinburgh.

Age 98: Fred Streeter, English broadcaster and gardener, was still answering hundreds of thousands of gardening letters.

Age 99: Dora Booth, a major in the Salvation Army and granddaughter of General Booth, took part in a TV talk show with Russell Harty. When asked if, had her grandfather been alive, he would have come on TV, she replied, "No, he would have been doing something more important."

Age 100: Estelle Winwood, English-born actress who appeared in forty Broadway plays and many films, was living in California, smoking sixty cigarettes a day, drinking sherry, and playing bridge most evenings. She had been married four times. At 100, she said she was "still waiting for something wonderful to happen."

Source: Book of Ages, Desmond Morris, 1983

Burial places of the famous

Many of the great and the good in British history have ended up at Westminster Abbey, but quite a few managed to leave their bones or ashes elsewhere.

Queen Boudicea of the Iceni, died 61 AD: under platform 10, King's Cross Station, London. Probably true–she was killed in battle by the Romans on the site of what is now the station.

King Arthur: under the ruins of Glastonbury Abbey, allegedly.

The Venerable Bede: Durham Cathedral. Definitely.

King Canute: Winchester Cathedral.

William the Conqueror: St. Stephen's Church, Caen, Normandy.

Henry VIII: St George's Chapel, Windsor Castle, Berks, beside his third wife, Jane Seymour.

Samuel Pepys: St. Olave's Church, Hart Street, City of London, alongside his wife, Elizabeth.

Queen Victoria: Royal Mausoleum, Frogmore, Windsor, Berks.

Napoleon III, Emperor of the French: Abbey Church, St. Michael, Farnborough, Hampshire.

Benjamin Disraeli: St. Michael's Churchyard, Hughenden, Bucks.

Winston Churchill: St. Martin's Churchyard, Bladon, Oxfordshire.

Horatio Nelson: St. Paul's Cathedral, London.

Jeremy Bentham, philosopher and social reformer: University College, London, where his embalmed body is kept in a showcase.

Karl Marx: Highgate New Cemetery, London.

Michael Faraday: Highgate Old Cemetery, London.

George Stephenson: Trinity Church, Chesterfield, Derbyshire.

Shakespeare: Holy Trinity Church, Stratford-upon-Avon.

Jane Austen: Winchester Cathedral.

Mrs. Beeton: Norwood Cemetery, London.

Samuel Taylor Coleridge: St. Michael's Church, Highgate, London.

Sir Arthur Conan Doyle: All Saints Churchyard, Minstead, Hampshire.

Lewis Carroll: Guildford Cemetery, Surrey.

Charlotte Brontë: St. Michael and All Angels Church, Haworth, Yorkshire; also sister Emily. Anne is buried at St. Mary's Churchyard, Castle Road, Scarborough.

T. S. Eliot: St. Michael's Church, East Coker, Somerset.

D. H. Lawrence: Eastwood Cemetery, Notts.

George Orwell: All Saints, Sutton Courtney, Oxon.

John Ruskin: St. Andrew's Churchyard, Coniston, Cumbria.

Percy Bysshe Shelley: St. Peter's Churchyard, Bournemouth, Dorset, where his heart was reinterred after his death by drowning in Italy.

Virginia Woolf: Monks House, Rodmell, Sussex, where her ashes were buried in the garden.

Beatrix Potter: Near Sawrey, Cumbria. Her ashes were scattered in a field by her shepherd and the exact location was never revealed.

Florence Nightingale: St. Margaret's Churchyard, East Wellow, Hampshire. Only her initials, F. N., appear on her tombstone.

Source: Who's Buried Where in England: A Constable Guide, *1982*

Food quotations

Great food inventions

Top diets in the U.S.

Top American sandwich towns

Consumer concerns

American food days

Wrapping rage

Five food anecdotes

FOOD
AND
DRINK

Food quotations

Tell me what you eat, and I will tell you what you are.
ANTHELME BRILLAT-SAVARIN (1755–1826),
The Physiology of Taste, 1825

The most remarkable thing about my mother is that for thirty years she served the family nothing but leftovers. The original meal has never been found.
CALVIN TRILLIN (1935–)

He who comes first, eats first.
[Familiar as: *First come first served.*]
EIKE VON REPKOW (~1220), *Sachsenspiegel*

Preach not to others what they should eat, but eat as becomes you, and be silent.
EPICTETUS (55–135)

Food is an important part of a balanced diet.
FRAN LEBOWITZ (1950–)

What some call health, if purchased by perpetual anxiety about diet, isn't much better than tedious disease.
GEORGE DENNISON PRENTICE (1802–1870)

Part of the secret of success in life is to eat what you like and let the food fight it out inside.
MARK TWAIN (1835–1910)

Never eat more than you can lift.
MISS PIGGY

*Ask not what you can do for your country.
Ask what's for lunch.*
ORSON WELLES (1915–1985)

There are people who strictly deprive themselves of each
and every eatable, drinkable, and smokable which has
in any way acquired a shady reputation. They pay
this price for health. And health is all they get for it.
How strange it is. It is like paying out your whole
fortune for a cow that has gone dry.

MARK TWAIN (1835–1910)

Fish is the only food that is considered spoiled
once it smells like what it is.

P. J. O'ROURKE (1947–)

You can tell a lot about a fellow's character
by his way of eating jellybeans.

RONALD REAGAN (1911–2004),
quoted in the *Observer*, March 29, 1981

I've been on a diet for two weeks
and all I've lost is two weeks.

TOTIE FIELDS (1930–1978)

Source: www.quotationspage.com

Great food inventions

Here's a list of foods we take for granted, and who invented them.

Croissant
The French are generally credited with reinventing the croissant dough in its current form, especially as it's a French word meaning crescent or crescent-shaped, and the first recipes appeared in the early twentieth century. But, according to one legend, a Polish soldier invented the croissant in 1683 in Vienna, during the war between Austria and Turkey.

Frozen foods

Lovers of frozen foods can thank an American taxidermist, Clarence Birdseye from Brooklyn, New York, for them. Having seen people in the Arctic preserving fresh fish and meat in barrels of seawater, which became quickly frozen, Birdseye realized that rapid freezing meant food would still be fresh when it was later thawed and cooked. In 1923 he spent seven dollars on an electric fan, buckets of brine, and cakes of ice. Six years later he sold his patents and trademarks for twenty-two million dollars. Quick frozen foods first went on sale in 1930, in Massachusetts.

Hamburger

Who exactly invented the hamburger–and when–is still up for debate. German immigrants probably brought the hamburger patty to the United States in the nineteenth century, but as for inventing the hamburger–some say it was fifteen-year-old Charles Nagreen in 1885 at a county fair in Wisconsin, others that it was Frank Menches in 1892 at a county fair in Ohio. Either way, it would be a good few decades before the trademark for the name "cheeseburger" was awarded, to Louis Ballast of the Humpty Dumpty Drive-In, Denver, Colorado in 1935. Meanwhile, the slugburger–a deep fat-fried beef mixture–has its very own annual festival in Mississippi each July.

Hot dogs

Again, the origins can be traced back to German immigrants, who introduced the wienerwurst, or wiener, to the United States. But it was a catering director at New York City's Polo Grounds who put the hot dog into a bun–although some say the inventor was Charles Feltman at Coney Island amusement park. As for where the term hot dog came from, some attribute it to a nineteenth-century American sports cartoonist who caricatured Germans as dachshund dogs. His cartoons alleged that cheap wieners sold at Coney Island had dog meat, and in 1913 the term "hot dog" was officially banned from signs on the Island. The term first appeared in print in 1900.

HP Sauce

This popular British condiment was apparently created by a chef at the British Houses of Parliament, hence its name, but the recipe was invented by a Nottingham shopkeeper who traded it with a vinegar company in order to settle a debt. It's also known as "Wilson's Gravy," after Harold Wilson, Labour Prime Minister of the 1960s and 1970s, who was said to cover his food with HP Sauce.

Ice-cream cone

Italo Marchiony, an Italian who immigrated to New York City in the 1800s, was granted a patent for the ice cream cone in 1903–he claimed he had created the cone in 1896. But cones were also independently introduced at the 1904 St. Louis World's Fair, where they were sold for the first time, and many credit Charles Menches with the invention. When Menches ran out of ice cream dishes he borrowed the cone idea from another stallholder, Ernest Hamwi, a Syrian who was selling Zalabia, a Middle Eastern wafer-like pastry. However, there were fifty other ice-cream vendors at the fair, and several also claimed the invention for themselves.

Iced tea

Invented by Richard Blechyden, an Englishman selling beverages at the St. Louis World's Fair in 1904.

Instant mashed potatoes

Invented by a Canadian, Edward A. Asselbergs, in 1962.

Marmite

A German chemist first found that spent brewer's yeast could be made into a concentrated food product, but it wasn't until 1902 that a British company managed to manufacture the yeast extract for commercial purposes. The Marmite Food Company initially rented a disused brewery in Burton-on-Trent and later extended operations to London. Marmite's popularity was boosted in 1912 with the discovery of vitamins–the yeast in Marmite providing a good source of vitamin B. Marmite was served to British soldiers during both world wars.

Pasta
Pasta might be regarded as the all-Italian food, but it originated in China around forty centuries ago, and wasn't introduced to Italy until 1291 AD. The first documented recipe for pasta was in a Sicilian cookery book in 1000. In the 1800s pasta began to be combined with tomato-based sauces, and a variety of new shapes took off. "Lasagna" (lasagne) may come from the Greek "lasanon," meaning a chamber pot.

Pizza
The invention of modern pizza is often attributed to a Naples baker in the 1800s, but an earlier form of pizza had been eaten for centuries in many Mediterranean countries. The earliest pizza shop was reportedly opened in 1830 in Naples, while the first pizzeria in North America was opened in New York City in 1905.

Popcorn
Popcorn goes back a very long way. In 1948 two American scientists discovered ears of popcorn in a cave in New Mexico, which were carbon dated to be about 5,600 years old. Ancient popcorn poppers have also been found in Peru, dating back to pre-Inca times.

In the sixteenth century popcorn was an important food for the Aztec Indians, and in the seventeenth century Native Americans reportedly brought popcorn with them to meetings with English colonists. The first machine to pop popcorn was invented in Chicago in 1885, and the first brand-name popcorn in the United States, named Jolly Time, was launched in 1914. Popcorn saw a rise in popularity with the opening of movie theaters in the early twentieth century and again when television took off in the 1950s.

Powdered milk
The Mongolians are said to be the first to have produced powdered milk, back in the thirteenth century. They added millet and ice to milk, boiled it until it thickened, and then let it dry.

Sandwich
Invented by Englishman John Montagu, the Earl of Sandwich, who wanted a meal that could be eaten with one hand so that he wouldn't have to interrupt his gambling at cards.

Tomato ketchup
"Ketchup" originally comes from the Chinese "ke-stiap," a pickled fish sauce. F. & J. Heinz Company began selling tomato ketchup in 1876.

Vegemite
A yeast product similar to Marmite. The spread was invented by an Australian scientist and, after a national competition to find a name, was launched in 1923. During the Second World War both military and civilian populations had Vegemite in their rations. In 1935 the recipe and manufacturing methods were sold to the American company Kraft Foods. Nowadays, nine out of ten Australian households have a jar of Vegemite in the pantry.

Sources:
www.thinkquest.org
www.globalgourmet.com
www.inventors.about.com
www.lapiazzaonline.com
www.homecooking.about.com
www.ilovemarmite.com
www.danielroy.tripod.com
www.whatscookingamerica.net

Top diets in the U.S.

Internet searches for the perfect diet are popular year round, but especially just after New Year, according to the Internet search engine Lycos. It ranks the following diets and diet products as its Top 10 for 2002. Big name diets like Weight Watchers came top in the United States, but in Canada a popular search was for "apple cider vinegar," since pills made from the vinegar allegedly promote weight loss.

1. Weight Watchers	6. Body for Life
2. Atkins Diet	7. Richard Simmons
3. Metabolife	8. Hollywood Diet
4. Zone Diet	9. Jenny Craig
5. Mayo Clinic Diet	10. Slim Fast

Top American sandwich towns

The following U.S. towns have been rated by the Oscar Mayer Company, famous for its bologna sandwiches, according to the consumption rate in each place:

1. Philadelphia
2. Baltimore
3. Pittsburgh
4. Los Angeles/Long Beach
5. Long Island
6. Seattle/Everest
7. Tampa/St. Petersburg
8. Detroit
9. Atlanta
10. Dallas/Fort Worth

Consumer concerns

Barely a month goes by without one food hazard warning or another–whether salmonella, dye contamination, or donkey meat in salami. But while UK consumers remain worried about genetically modified (GM) foods, they are far less worried than they used to be about mad cow disease.

Concern	2000	2003
Mad cow disease	61%	42%
Raw meat	70%	63%
Eggs	26%	20%
GM foods	43%	38%

Consumers also seem a lot more educated, with 78% claiming to check food labels:

	2000	2003
Aware we should eat five portions of fruit and vegetables a day	43%	59%
Actually eat the five portions	26%	28%
Look for total salt content in a product	22%	36%

Shopping and eating habits
50% of consumers shop about once a week
95% shop at supermarkets
Six out of ten enjoy cooking
40% cook meals from raw or fresh ingredients once a day
50% sit down once a day for their main meal
    with household members

Source: Food Standards Agency
Consumer Attitudes to Food Survey

American food days

The British may have Pancake Day, but that's nothing compared to the "national" food days celebrated by Americans, many of which are tied to brand names:

Prune Breakfast Month–January
National Potato Chip Day–March 14
National Egg Salad Week–April 12–18
National Cheeseball Day–April 17
National Hamburger Month–May
National Iced Tea Month–June
National Baked Bean Month–July
National Cotton Candy Day–December 7
National Lemon Cupcake Day–December 15
National Chocolate Covered Anything Day–December 16
National Bicarbonate of Soda Day–December 30

Wrapping rage

Each year in the UK 67,000 people injure themselves while trying to do something as apparently simple as open a can of beans or unwrap a sandwich.

The 10 worst things to open
Tops of bleach bottles
and toilet cleaners

Shrink-wrapped cheese and ham

Sealed sandwich packages

Pull-top cans

Tins of meat and fish

Milk and juice cartons

Childproof tops
on medicine bottles

Cellophane tops
on microwave ready meals

Soap powder boxes

Cookies

Source: survey conducted for Yours *magazine*

Five food anecdotes

J. M. Barrie was once at a dinner party sitting next to George Bernard Shaw, who was a noted vegetarian. Shaw had requested a special dish of salad and his favorite dressing. When the unpleasant-looking plate of food arrived, Barrie whispered to Shaw, "Tell me, have you eaten that–or are you going to?"

Handel, the great German composer who lived for many years in England, sent word to a local tavern, booking dinner for two. When he arrived, on his own, the landlord begged his pardon and said he thought that Mr. Handel was expecting company. "I am the company," said Handel, and ate his way through the dinner for two.

Alfred Hitchcock, the film director, was noted for his fondness for food. At one dinner party he considered the helpings he had been served to be totally inadequate. As Hitchcock was leaving, the host said to him, "I do hope you will dine with us again soon." "By all means," replied Hitchcock. "How about now . . . ?"

Eleanor Roosevelt, wife of U.S. President Franklin Delano Roosevelt, was very fond of sweetbreads. In one week they appeared on the White House menu six times. The president eventually wrote a note to his wife: "I am getting to the point where my stomach rebels and this does not help my relations with foreign ministers. I hit two of them today."

William Makepeace Thackeray, while on a lecture tour of the United States, was invited to a feast of best American oysters by his U.S. publisher, James T. Fields. He was overcome by the sight of their size and asked how he should devour them. Fields swallowed his in one gulp. Thackeray eventually got up the courage to do the same. Asked how it felt, Thackeray replied, "As if I had swallowed a baby."

The Twelve Days of Christmas

The rules of society: 1860

Food requirements, Victorian era

Factory rules

Management of the infant

Mourning clothes

Victorian underclothes

Advice for a good WAAF

HISTORY

The Twelve Days of Christmas

Catholics in England during the period 1558-1839 were prohibited by law from any practice of their faith, public or otherwise. According to a popular urban myth, "The Twelve Days of Christmas" was written as a Catechism Song to help young Catholics memorize the tenets of their faith and avoid being caught with anything in writing.

The **True Love** referred to God himself, the **Me** to every baptized person.

The **Partridge in a Pear Tree** is Jesus Christ the Son of God. In the song, Christ is symbolically presented as a mother partridge, which feigns injury to decoy predators from her helpless nestlings, an expression of Christ's sadness over the fate of Jerusalem.

The **Two Turtle Doves** are the Old and the New Testaments.

The **Three French Hens** are Faith, Hope, and Charity, the theological virtues.

The **Four Calling Birds** are the four Gospels and/or the four Evangelists.

The **Five Golden Rings** are the first five books of the Old Testament, which give the history of "man's" fall from grace.

Six Geese a'Laying are the six days of Creation.

Seven Swans a'Swimming are the seven gifts of the Holy Spirit, the seven sacraments.

Eight Maids a'Milking are the eight beatitudes.

Nine Ladies Dancing are the nine fruits of the Holy Spirit.

Ten Lords a'Leaping are the Ten Commandments.

Eleven Pipers Piping are the eleven faithful apostles.

Twelve Drummers Drumming are the twelve points of doctrine of the Apostles' Creed.

Source: Cumbrian church newsletter

The rules of society: 1860

Social intercourse in the Victorian era was fraught with unspoken rules, especially in terms of visiting. A domestic manual recommended the following:

"Those who mix in society are in the habit of reminding one another of their existence, either by personally calling on each other during certain hours, or by merely leaving their cards at the door."

The visits were made chiefly by ladies and idle men, usually between the hours of 1 and 5 (or 12 and 4 in the country). A call was to last between 15 and 20 minutes and was made at least twice a year and on the following occasions:

1. After the birth of a baby–either in person or by sending a servant
2. On the marriage of a daughter–usually the day after the wedding
3. After a death–no calls were made until the lady of the house had sent round her cards "to return thanks for the inquiries" made during the time of mourning
4. Prior to a long absence from home–ladies then called on their friends

Further advice

When the lady making a call is married to a gentleman too busy to make the call with her, it is sufficient if she leaves his card for the master of the house.

In leaving cards for a married couple, a lady usually leaves one card and a gentleman two.

Formal calls on particular occasions should be returned within a few days, "failing which an apology is due."

Refreshments don't have to be offered to callers in town, but should in country districts when the caller has come a considerable distance.

Food requirements, Victorian era

Meat and potatoes, along with a pint of malt liquor a day, were regarded as the most important part of a good diet for Victorian men.

Average daily amount of the best kind of food required by an adult male

Meat	¾lb
Bread	¾lb
Potatoes	1½lb
(or green vegetables)	
Cheese	2oz
Butter	1oz
Milk	2oz
Sugar	1oz
Tea	½oz
Coffee	1oz
Malt liquor	1 pint

Cheap food, sufficient to support an adult in good health

Bread	1lb
Potatoes	2lb
Peas or beans	4oz
Dripping or lard	4oz
Cabbage or greens	1lb
Cheese	3oz

Various kinds of cheap food suitable to the poor man

Bullock's, pig's, calf's or sheep's liver, melt or kidney
Pig's blood for black puddings
Inferior pieces of beef

Sheep's trotters
Sheep's head and pluck
Cheap fish
Peas and beans
Mushrooms

Factory rules

Factory conditions were notoriously hard in Victorian England, and workers constantly ran the risk of being fined. Here's a list of rules that had to be obeyed in a Lancashire cotton mill in 1851:

Rules to be observed by the hands employed in this mill
Any person coming too late shall be fined as follows:
    for 5 minutes 2d, 10 minutes 4d, and 15 minutes 6d

For waste on the floor 2d

For any oil wasted or spilled on the floor 2d each offence, besides paying for the value of the oil

Any person found leaving their work and found talking with any other of the workpeople shall be fined 2d for each offence

For every oath or insolent language, 3d for the first offence, and, if repeated, they shall be dismissed

All persons in our employ shall serve four weeks notice before leaving their employ; but L. Whitaker and Sons shall and will turn any person off without notice being given

The Masters would recommend that all their workpeople wash themselves every morning, but they shall wash themselves at least twice every week, Monday morning and Thursday morning: and any found not washed will be fined 3d for each offence

Any person willfully damaging this notice will be dismissed

Source: Victorian Life and Transport, *Richard Dunning, 1981*

Management of the infant

If you thought detailed lists of everything required for newborn babies was a twenty-first-century trend, then consider the advice contained in an 1857 *Manual of Domestic Economy*:

Articles required for infant management
1. A low chair, with or without rockers
2. A footstool
3. Two thick flannel aprons
4. One large washing basin
5. One soap-dish and soap (best yellow or white curd)
6. One small enamel saucepan
7. One semi-porcelain pipkin and lamp
8. One pap-boat (silver or crockery)
9. One feeding-bottle, with two or three nipples
10. One small jug
11. One teaspoon and one dessert-spoon
12. One small pot de chamber, with two flannel covers

The above list was intended for a baby's first month. The semi-porcelain pipkin and lamp was "a most useful modern invention" used to warm water and food. The pap-boat was used to "force" the baby to take disagreeables, either in the shape of food or medicine. The nipples on the feeding bottle should be India-rubber, preferred to the traditional hollowed-out cow teat or sewn-up wash-leather–both of which were liable to become semiputrid.

Mourning clothes

When it came to mourning the passing of a loved one, Victorian women had to follow a strict protocol, whereas men could normally get away with a hatband and a black suit.

Wife for husband
One year, one month: bombazine covered with crepe; widow's cap, lawn cuffs, collars

Daughter for parent
Six months: black with black or white crepe (for young girls); no linen cuffs and collars; no jewelry for first two months

Mother for child
Six months: black with crepe; no linen cuffs and collars; no jewelry for first two months

Mother for infant
Three months, often with no crepe

Wife for husband's parents
Eighteen months in black bombazine with crepe

Victorian underclothes

Victorian women were "incredibly modest," recalls Gwen Raverat, one chronicler of the times. "You could see a friend in her petticoat, but nothing below that was considered decent." While "decent" women didn't take much trouble with their underclothes, these garments could be complicated, favoring the layered method of dress. In her 1952 memoir, Raverat describes sharing a room one night with a young lady who was wearing the following underclothes:

1. Thick, long-legged, long-sleeved woollen combinations
2. Over them, white cotton combinations, with plenty of buttons and frills
3. Very serious, bony, gray stays, with suspenders
4. Black woollen stockings
5. White cotton drawers, with buttons and frills

6. White cotton "petticoat-bodice," with embroidery, buttons and frills
7. Rather short, white flannel petticoat
8. Long alpaca petticoat, with a flounce round the bottom
9. Pink flannel blouse

Source: Gwen Raverat (1885–1957) wood engraver and illustrator, granddaughter of Charles Darwin, quoted in The Victorian House, *Judith Flanders, 2003*

Advice for a good WAAF

In 1940 Deirdre Byer was already in the Women's Air Force, helping to win the war. Her younger sister, Elizabeth, was just about to join up–so Deirdre wrote her a list, telling her what she should bring and what she might expect:

2 prs pajamas

1 dressing gown

1 pr slippers

Toilet things in a waterproof bag

Makeup

Natural nail varnish

Large duster

1 small brush (for boots)

1 small brush (cleaning buttons)

1 button stick

1 large tin Silvo

Large tin Cherry Blossom–this will
shortly be rationed

Large supply of paper, ink, envelopes,
and stamps if desirous of not giving
up friends (male)

Two black ties–if you can obtain them
without coupons

Some fine hairnets with elastic–to
keep your hair off your collar

Hairbrush, comb, grips

Soap and towel–there is a plain one of
mine in my drawer, but don't you dare
get it swiped

DO'S

Accept all garments given you on kitting-out parade,
even if they don't fit you, even if you don't wear them, as
you will have to produce them on kit inspection.

When cleaning buttons, put button stick through
buttons, apply Silvo heavily, and burn with a match. The
Silvo will run off in a thick brown liquid. Apply more
Silvo, allow to dry, and brush well. Finish off with the
duster. Do cap badge in similar manner.

DON'TS

Wear your hat on one side.

Wear your stockings inside out.

Never cut a service article of clothing.

Forget to clean buttons and shoes.

Don't take anything of value–it will be swiped.

Don't get downhearted.

There is only one "don't" I have forgotten. I should have
told you ages ago. Don't join the forces . . .

Strange things sent through the mail

Body decoration

Fear of flying

Job applications

Dollar billionaires

Excuses for late payment

Top hobbies

Most common dreams

Weird phobias

Office romance

Personal ads

Most popular names

Wish list

PEOPLE'S
FUNNY
WAYS

Strange things sent through the mail

The National Return Letter Centre in the UK deals with millions of undeliverable letters each year—of which a quarter are said to be successfully redelivered. Here's a list of some of the stranger things sent through the mail.

A live snake

A mummified hand

A putrid salmon

Thousands of Christmas cards without addresses

An old-fashioned wooden leg

Thousands of Valentine's cards without addresses

£25,000 cash in an envelope (accidentally mailed, it was supposed to go into the night safe of a big department store via internal mail)

Lots of underwear

Letters addressed to fictional characters—Santa Claus, Peggy Mitchell, Dot Cotton (both television characters)

Letters, without addresses, to famous athletes

Source: article in the Guardian

Body decoration

One in five Britons now has a tattoo—with men preferring their arm tattooed and women opting for their back, shoulder, or leg. But even more people—48 percent according to a survey in the *Observer*—now have a piercing somewhere on their body. Pierced genitals are just as popular as pierced eyebrows.

Most popular places for tattoos	Percentage
Arms	51
Back	30
Shoulders	27
Legs	17
Breasts/chest	10
Bottom	9
Stomach	7
Hands	6
Neck	4
Feet	3
Other	3

Most popular places for piercing	Percentage
Ears	94
Navel	11
Nose	7
Nipples	4
Tongue	4
Eyebrow	3
Genitals	3
Lips	3

Source: Observer *survey*

Fear of flying

Fear of flying is one of the most common fears there is. People know it's largely irrational, but that doesn't make it any easier to bear. Those who fear flying are also likely to fear heights, are petrified of being driven by another car driver, and are pretty scared of boats. However, they tend not to fear train rides at all.

The following comes from a survey of those who suffer from fear of flying.

Percentage who also suffer from:

Panic attacks	11
Claustrophobia	22
Fear of heights	67
Fear of driving	11
Fear of being driven by some other drivers	89
Fear of being driven by all other drivers	22
Fear of trains	0
Fear of boats	44
Fear of lifts	33
Fear of escalators	11
Fear of fairground rides	78

And here's self-help guru Allen Carr's advice on how to conquer a fear of flying for good.

Follow all the instructions

Keep an open mind

Start off in a happy frame of mind

Think positively

Go for it!

Enjoy it!

Do not try to take your mind off the flight

You are going to take control

Don't try to fly the plane!

Source: The Easy Way to Enjoy Flying, *Allen Carr, 2000*

Job applications

The list below contains excerpts from résumés and cover letters . . .

1. "I have lurnt Word Perfect 6.0 computor and spreasheet progroms."
2. "Am a perfectionist and rarely if ever forget details."
3. "Received a plague for Salesperson of the Year."
4. "Wholly responsible for two (2) failed financial institutions."
5. "Reason for leaving last job: maturity leave."
6. "Failed bar exam with relatively high grades."
7. "It's best for employers that I not work with people."
8. "Let's meet, so you can 'ooh' and 'aah' over my experience."
9. "I was working for my mum until she decided to move."
10. "Marital status: single. Unmarried. Unengaged. Uninvolved. No commitments."
11. "I have an excellent track record, although I am not a horse."
12. "I am loyal to my employer at all costs. Please feel free to respond to my resume on my office voicemail."
13. "My goal is to be a meteorologist. But since I possess no training in meteorology, I suppose I should try stockbroking."
14. "I procrastinate, especially when the task is unpleasant."
15. "Personal interests: donating blood. Fourteen gallons so far."
16. "Instrumental in ruining entire operation for a chain store."
17. "Note: Please don't misconstrue my 14 jobs as 'job-hopping.' I have never quit a job."
18. "Marital status: often. Children: various."
19. "The company made me a scapegoat, just like my three previous employers."
20. "Finished eighth in my class of ten."
21. "References: none. I've left a path of destruction behind me."

Dollar billionaires

London has the highest number of dollar billionaires in the world. The following is a list of dollar billionaires throughout the world in 2004.

London	40
New York	31
Moscow	23
Geneva	20
Los Angeles	18
Hong Kong	16
San Francisco	15
Dallas	14
Tokyo	10
Paris	10
Mexico City	9
Seattle	9
Chicago	7
Boston	6
Palm Beach	6
Singapore	6
Taipei	6
Hamburg	5
Toronto	5
Milan	2

Source: Sunday Times

Excuses for late payment

Anyone who has dealings with companies knows it can take ages to receive payment for services rendered. A survey by the Better Payment Practice Group found that the most common excuse given for late payment was that the company was waiting for the check to be signed. More imaginative excuses included the assertion that the checkbook had been buried, along with its deceased owner.

Most common excuses for late payment	Percentage
1. Waiting for the check to be signed	23
2. Lost the invoice, send a copy	22
3. Cash-flow problems, waiting for debtors to pay us	16
4. Account handler is off sick or is unavailable	15
5. Check is in the mail	6
6. New computer system being installed or has failed	6
7. Waiting for new checkbook or have run out of checks	5
8. Invoice in dispute	3
9. We pay on 60/90 days, not 30 days	2
10. You've missed the payment run	2

More bizarre excuses

"The checkbook has been destroyed in the flood."

"The owner's been buried with his checkbook."

"The director went for an operation and never returned, as he went off with the nurse."

"The tide is out and the director is unable to get in to pay checks."

"I cannot make payment until the planets are aligned, which is only twice a year."

"We're in the middle of an armed robbery."

"Not now, it's the office party."

Top hobbies

Londoners would rather be at the pub than join a yoga class or engage in charity work, but their favorite leisure activity is eating out. Cooking, gardening, and do-it-yourself have also become more popular, due to the increase in lifestyle television shows. Less than 2 percent of people have given yoga a try, but 9 percent regularly attend Bingo sessions.

Top 10 London hobbies
1. Eating out
2. Reading
3. Foreign travel
4. Pub
5. Cookery
6. Gardening
7. Fashion
8. DIY
9. Cinema
10. Gym

Source: Report by marketing solutions company CACI

Most common dreams

The average person spends a quarter of each night dreaming–which adds up to about six years of their life. The most vivid dreams happen during a type of sleep called Rapid Eye Movement (REM) when the brain is very active and the eyes move back and forth under the lids.

The ancient Greeks believed that dreams could reveal important things about our health. Recent research has shown that people who say they never dream have the highest mortality rate.

**Top 10 most common dreams in the
eighties, according to *Prediction* magazine**
1. Houses
2. Water
3. Airplanes
4. Snakes
5. Doors
6. Eyes
7. A tower
8. A tree
9. Teeth
10. Mountains

Top 10 most common dreams in 2004

Falling is one of today's most common dreams. It can
mean the dreamer fears losing respect, or can indicate
money problems. If you land and wake suddenly then this
is a "wake-up call" to attend to matters in the physical
world.

Dreaming about a house is another very common dream.
A house usually represents yourself, with rooms
representing different aspects. Doors are opportunities.

Car dreams are also common. The meaning depends on:
Who is driving? Is it a pleasant journey? What is the state
of the car? Cars are a symbol of power, status, and vitality.

Animals: wild animals denote fear and even misfortune.
Domestic animals usually mean good fortune.

Celebrities: people don't dream as much about God or the
Devil anymore, instead they dream about meeting or
becoming a famous person. These tend to be happy,
positive dreams suggesting that a goal can finally be
achieved.

Being chased: a dream linked to anxiety, which suggests the dreamer is running away from something. If you escape the chase then your life quest is taking a new road.

Death: although scary, dreaming about someone else's or your own death can actually signify that a rebirth is about to occur in your life.

Flying: this indicates the dreamer is trying to exercise free choice in their life.

Being lost: the meaning is literal–you are lost in your life, adrift.

Being naked in a public place: clothes symbolize your outer expression, being naked can suggest you are letting down the walls that surround you.

People's tastes in reading also affect dreams. The results of a Dream Lab experiment, which surveyed 100,000 people, showed:

Readers of fiction have the most bizarre dreams.

People who read romance books are more likely to tell their dreams to other people.

There is no relation between reading crime or thriller books and having nightmares.

People who sleep for long hours go to a library more often than those whose sleep is short.

Sources:
www.webspawner.com
www.saga.co.uk
www.kindredspirit.co.uk

Weird phobias

At least a quarter of people are said to be affected by one kind of phobia or another, often a fear of spiders or heights. Here are some lesser-known fears:

Alektorophobia–fear of chickens
Alliumphobia–fear of garlic
Anthrophobia–fear of flowers
Arachibutyrophobia–fear of peanut butter sticking to the roof of the mouth
Athazagoraphobia–a fear of forgetting things
Automatonophobia–fear of ventriloquists' dummies
Batophobia–fear of being close to high buildings
Bogyphobia–fear of the bogeyman
Chronophobia–fear of time
Cnidophobia–fear of string
Coulrophobia–fear of clowns
Deipnophobia–fear of dinner conversations
Ergasiophobia–a fear of work
Geniophobia–fear of chins
Hellenologophobia–a fear of Greek words and scientific terms
Hippopotomonstrosesquippedaliophobia–fear of long words
Lachanophobia–fear of vegetables
Mageirocophobia–fear of cooking
Metrophobia–fear of poetry
Ostraconophobia–fear of shellfish
Panophobia–fear of everything
Phobophobia–fear of fear
Pogonophobia–a fear of beards
Pteronophobia–fear of being tickled by feathers
Rupophobia–a fear of dirt
Triskaidekaphobia–a fear of the number 13
Xanthophobia–a fear of the color yellow

Office romance

People who work in marketing or advertising have a pretty good chance of an affair with a work colleague–unlike architects, who are more likely to keep business and pleasure separate.

A study by Tiscali.co.uk, the Internet service provider, found that most people began their relationship by flirting in the hallway at work.

Percentage of people who have had a romantic involvement with a work colleague

Marketing/Advertising	93
Pharmaceuticals	85
Telecoms	73
Financial Services	69
Sales	62
Accounting	59
Law	57
IT	54
Broadcasting	52
Education	51
Retail	50
Banking	50
Design	49
Property	49
Media/TV	48
Social Services	48
Leisure	48
Hotels	47
Publishing	47
Tourism/Travel Agents	46
Events	46
Insurance	46
Office Administration	46
Recruitment	45
Civil Service	44
Charity	43

Internet/New Media   41
Research   34
Architecture   33

Personal ads

How many people tell the truth when they are searching, or advertising, for a soulmate? The following list is a guide to what might be behind people's descriptions of themselves:

Women seeking Men

40-ish = 48
Adventurous = Has had more partners than you ever will
Affectionate = Possessive
Artist = Unreliable
Commitment-minded = Pick out curtains, now
Communication important = Just try to get a word in edgewise
Consistent = Fifteenth ad placed this year
Fun = Annoying
Light drinker = Lush

Men seeking Women

40-ish = 52 and looking for 25 year old
Artist = Delicate ego badly in need of massage
Educated = Will aways treat you like an idiot
Fun = Good with a remote and a six pack
Honest = Pathological liar
Like romantic walks on the beach = Reads *Cosmo* and thinks this is what you want to hear
Physically fit = Spends a lot of time in front of mirrors admiring himself
Sensitive = Needy

Source: The House of Lists (*Web site*)

Most popular names

After six years, the name Chloe has finally been knocked off the top spot by Emily, now the UK's most popular girl's name–and the most popular name in the United States since 1996.

In terms of boys' names, Jack has been the most popular for nine years–it remains popular in Northern Ireland, Scotland, the Republic of Ireland, and New Zealand, but far less so in the U.S. and Australia.

The rise in the popularity of Alfie is attributed to a character in the UK TV soap *EastEnders*, while the rise in the girl's name Chardonnay is attributed to a character in the UK TV drama *Footballer's Wives*.

The most popular baby names in the UK, 2003

Male	*Female*
Jack	Emily
Joshua	Ellie
Thomas	Chloe
James	Jessica
Daniel	Sophie

The list above comes from the National Statistics Office, but consider the top names of 2003 according to the Web site BabyNames.com:

Male	*Female*
Aidan	Madison
Jaden	Emma
Caden	Abigail
Ethan	Riley
Caleb	Chloe

Historically, John is one of the longest-running favorite boys' names dating back to 1800, while Sarah has been one of the top girls' names for almost 200 years.

Top names in the UK, 1800

Male	Female
William	Mary
John	Ann
Thomas	Elizabeth
James	Sarah
George	Jane

In the U.S.

Male	Female
John	Mary
William	Anna
Charles	Elizabeth
George	Margaret
James	Minnie

Top names in the UK, 1900

Male	Female
William	Florence
John	Mary
George	Alice
Thomas	Annie
Charles	Elsie

In the U.S.

Male	Female
John	Mary
William	Helen
James	Anna
George	Margaret
Charles	Ruth

Top names in the UK, 1950

Male	Female
David	Susan
John	Linda
Peter	Margaret
Michael	Carol
Alan	Jennifer

In the U.S.

Male	Female
John	Linda
James	Mary
Robert	Patricia
William	Barbara
Michael	Susan

Top names in the UK, 1975

Male	Female
Stephen	Sarah
Mark	Nicole
Paul	Emma
Andrew	Joanne
David	Helen

In the U.S.

Male	Female
Michael	Jennifer
Christopher	Amy
Jason	Michelle
David	Heather
James	Angela
Robert (tie)	

Top names in the UK, 1988

Male	Female
Daniel	Rebecca
Christopher	Sarah
Michael	Emma
James	Laura
Matthew	Rachel

In the U.S.

Male	Female
Michael	Ashley
Christopher	Jessica
Matthew	Amanda
Joshua	Jennifer
David	Brittany

Sources:
For top UK names: www.worldzone.net (with credit to
The Guinness Book of Names) *and National Statistics Office.*
For top U.S. names: Social Security Administration, names taken from a survey of
Social Security Card applications (note: different spellings of similar names are
considered separate names in these tables).

Wish list

Water activities top the list when it comes to the things people want to do before they die. Swimming with dolphins is the number one dream, according to a BBC poll of 20,000 people. High on the list are physical challenges in far-off places, and getting in touch with animals. Number three on the list will remain the ultimate in wishful thinking, as the Concorde has now retired.

Swim with dolphins

Scuba dive on the Great Barrier Reef

Fly Concorde to New York

Go whale-watching

Dive with sharks

Skydive

Fly in a hot air balloon

Fly in a fighter jet

Go on safari

See the northern lights

Strange animal behavior

Top cats, United States

Top cat names

Top dog names

America's most popular dogs

Endangered species

African animal proverbs

Chinese animal proverbs

PETS

Strange animal behavior

"It's raining cats and dogs" might just be an expression, but there have been instances when it has rained fish and frogs. The probable reason is when minitornadoes scoop up water and small fish and then dump them on land. In 1976 Olympic yachts were even pelted by live maggots.

Falling fish

Aberdare, Mid Glamorgan	1841, 1859
Singapore	1861
Worcester	1881
Bournemouth	1948
Sunderland, Tyne, and Wear	1918
London	1984
Ipswich, Australia	1989
Great Yarmouth, Norfolk	2000

Falling frogs

Bedford	1979
Llanddewi, Wales	1996
Croydon, Surrey	1998, 2000

Falling turtle

Mississippi	1930

Falling corn

Evans, Colorado	1982-86

Falling alligators

South Carolina	1877

Sources: www.uktouristinfo.com, http://news.bbc.co.uk,
http://paranormal.miningco.com

Top cats, United States

According to the Cat Fanciers' Association, the trendiest cat in the United States last year was the Ragdoll, known for its tendency to go limp like a rag doll. However, the overall top five cat breeds in 2004 were:

1. Persian
2. Maine Coon
3. Exotic
4. Siamese
5. Abyssinian

Source: USA Weekend Magazine, *The American Kennel Club*

Top cat names, United States

	Male	Female
1.	Max	Sassy
2.	Sam	Misty
3.	Simba	Princess
4.	Charlie	Samantha
5.	Oliver	Lucy
6.	Oscar	Missy
7.	Gizmo	Molly
8.	Buddy	Sophie
9.	Toby	Pumpkin
10.	Spike	Maggie

Source: The American pet pharmacy 1800PetMeds

Top cat names, UK

The naming of cats is a difficult matter. A cat needs a name, that's particular, a name that's unusual, and more dignified, else how can he keep up his tail perpendicular?　　　　　T. S. ELIOT

More Britons now own cats than they do dogs. Many family pets are named after singing stars like Elvis and Britney. But some of the traditional favorites hark back to Latin–like the ever-popular Felix, which means "fortunate."

Top 5 cat names
1. Sooty
2. Tigger
3. Lucy
4. Smokey
5. Charlie

Source: www.petplanet.co.uk

Cat facts
40% of people say cats are their favorite pets (compared with 7% preferring dogs)

57% of people like cats because they are affectionate

49% like cats for their independence

46% like them because they are clean

27% say they like not having to exercise cats

Cats are most popular with the 35-44 age group (nearly a third of people in this age group own a cat)

67% of cat owners say curling up with their cat is the best way to deal with stress (preferable to speaking to a friend or going for a drink)

50% of people–both women and men–would rather wake up with their cat than their partner

98% of women would rather date someone who likes cats

Source: survey conducted by the Cats Protection League

Top dog names

Almost a quarter of UK households own a dog as a pet, spending on average $12.75 a week on food, bedding, and toys. Twenty-five years ago the most popular names for male dogs came from drinks, or famous dogs on TV or in film. Today many people give their dog a human name–with many named after soccer heroes like Becks and Zola.

Top 5 dog names, UK, 1980

Male	Female
1. Shep	1. Sheba
2. Brandy	2. Sally
3. Whisky	3. Rosie
4. Patch	4. Mandy
5. Butch	5. Tessa

Source: NCDL

Top 5 dog names, UK, 2004

Male	Female
1. Sam	1. Trixie
2. Spot	2. Polly
3. Pip	3. Jessie
4. Duke	4. Lucy
5. Piper	5. Bonnie

Source: PetPlanet

Top 5 dog names, U.S., 2004

Male	Female
1. Max	1. Maggie
2. Jake	2. Bear
3. Buddy	3. Molly
4. Bear	4. Shadow
5. Bailey	5. Lucy

Source: bowwow.com

America's most popular dogs

While British dog lovers are worried about the loss of traditional breeds, in the United States the concern is more about weight, as dogs are rapidly downsizing. The trendiest dog in America is now the Havanese, which can weigh just seven pounds. Small breeds are seen as just right for apartment living, and for traveling–although the Bernese mountain dog is third in the popularity stakes and it can weigh 120 pounds.

Top Dog Breeds, U.S., 2004
1. Labrador retriever (Canada)
2. Golden retriever
3. Beagle
4. German shepherd
5. Dachsund

Increase in popularity from 2003 to 2004
1. Havanese   up 28%
2. Cavalier King Charles spaniel   up 19%
3. Bernese mountain dog   up 14%

Fall in popularity from 2002 to 2004
1. Dalmatian   down 28%
2. Rottweiler   down 25%

Source: the Independent

Endangered species

Almost 1,000 species are now officially endangered in the United States–covering 985 animals and 597 plants.

Mammals	65
Birds	78
Reptiles	14
Amphibians	12
Fishes	71
Clams	62
Snails	21
Insects	35
Arachnids	12
Crustaceans	18
Flowering plants	569
Conifers, Cycads	2
Ferns, Allies	24
Lichens	2

Source: Threatened and Endangered Species System, U.S. Government

African animal proverbs

A dog knows the places he is thrown food.
Luyia, Western Kenya

A donkey knows no gratitude.
Swahili

A hyena cannot smell its own stench.
Kalenjin, Kenya

Dogs do not actually prefer bones to meat, it is just that no one ever gives them meat.
Akan, West Africa

He flees from the roaring lion to the crouching lion.
Sechuana

That man's a fool whose sheep flees twice.
Oji

The elephant never gets tired of carrying its tusks.
Vai, Liberia

The frog does not run in the daytime for nothing.
Igbo, Nigeria

Chinese animal proverbs

A bird in your hand is worth more than 100 in the forest.

How can you expect to find ivory in a dog's mouth?

Vicious as a tigress can be, she never eats her own cubs.

You can't catch a cub without going into the tiger's den.

You think you lost your horse? Who knows he may bring a whole herd back to you someday.

Source: www.famous-proverbs.com

World's top tourist destinations

World's costliest cities

Top Paris attractions

Most fascinating urinals

Odd town names

Most polluted parks in the U.S.

Stress in the cities, U.S.

Survey of U.S. cities

Top honeymoon destinations

Top 10 theme parks in the U.S.

Global weather extremes

Most destructive earthquakes

Most visited attractions in the UK

Top 5 lawns in the U.S.

PLACES

World's top tourist destinations

Destination	Visitors, in millions
France	76.5
Spain	49.5
United States	45.5
Italy	39.0
China	33.2
UK	23.4
Russia	21.1
Mexico	19.8
Canada	19.7
Austria	18.2

Source: World Tourism Organization, 2001 figures

World's costliest cities

Osaka/Kobe
Tokyo
Hong Kong
Libreville
Oslo
London
New York
Zurich
Singapore
Taipei
Tel Aviv

Source: Economist Intelligence Unit

Top Paris attractions

Here's a list of the attractions most visited in Paris, France. Museums remain the most popular, with 4 in the Top 6 for 2002:

Destination	Visitors, in millions
Eiffel Tower	6.2
Louvre Museum	5.7
Pompidou Centre	5.5
Cité des Sciences et de l'Industrie	2.5
Musée d'Orsay	2.1
Arc de Triomphe	1.4

Source: gofrance.about.com, Paris Office of Tourism Statistics

Most fascinating urinals

Do you have a favorite urinal? Perhaps you've even taken a photo of it. If so, then you can vote for the world's most fascinating urinals, and submit your illustration, at the Web site urinal.net. It ranks the following urinals as its Top 10:

1. Amundsen-Scott South Pole Station — South Pole, Antarctica
2. Hong Kong Sheraton Hotel and Towers — Hong Kong
3. Public Rest Rooms of Rothesay — Rothesay, Isle of Bute, UK
4. The Millennium Dome — London, England
5. Women's Urinal at Dairy Queen — Port Charlotte, Fla., U.S.
6. The Felix — Hong Kong
7. International Space Station — In Space
8. John Michael Kohler Arts Center — Sheboygan, Wis., U.S.
9. Madonna Inn — San Luis Obispo, Calif., U.S.
10. TV Hill — Kabul, Afghanistan

Odd town names

A town named Cool may not be that surprising in a state like California, but how about Intercourse in Pennsylvania? In England, town names often suggest sleepiness, like Great Snoring in Norfolk and Land of Nod in Devon.

Here's a selection of some of the odder town names in the UK, United States, and Canada.

UK
Brown Willey, Cornwall
California, Norfolk
Crackpot, North Yorks
Effingham, Surrey
Egypt, Hampshire
Eye, Suffolk
Foul Mile, East Sussex
Giggleswick, North Yorkshire
Great Snoring, Norfolk
Ham and Sandwich, Kent
Land of Nod, Devon
Little Snoring, Norfolk
Mousehole, Cornwall
Nasty, Hertfordshire
New Invention, Wales
North Piddle, Worcestershire
Pity Me, Co. Durham
Shop, Cornwall
Steeple Bumpstead,
   Cambridgeshire
Thong, Kent
Twatt, Orkney and Shetland
Wetwang With Fimber, Yorkshire
Windy Yet, Strathclyde, Scotland

U.S.
Normal, Alabama
Slapout, Alabama
Chicken, Alaska
Dead Horse, Alaska
Santa Claus, Arizona, Georgia,
   and Indiana
Why, Arizona
Toad Suck, Arkansas
Cool, California
Likely, California
Climax, Colorado, Georgia,
   Michigan, and Pennsylvania
Hygiene, Colorado
No Name, Colorado
Nowhere, Colorado
Paradox, Colorado
Cook's Hammock, Florida
Frostproof, Florida
Niceville, Florida
Between, Georgia
Experiment, Georgia
Hopeulikeit, Georgia
Po Biddy Crossroads, Georgia
Beer Bottle Crossing, Idaho

U.S. (continued)
Assumption, Illinois
Normal, Illinois
Bacon, Indiana
Loafers Station, Indiana
Surprise, Indiana
Smileyberg, Kansas
Big Bone Lick State Park,
   Kentucky
Cadillac, Kentucky
Chevrolet, Kentucky
Lovely, Kentucky
Ono, Kentucky
Ordinary, Kentucky
Waterproof, Louisiana
Accident, Maryland
Boring, Maryland
Hell, Michigan
Hells Creek Bottom, Mississippi
Hot Coffee, Mississippi
Money, Mississippi
Peculiar, Missouri

Tightwad, Missouri
Truth Or Consequences, New
   Mexico
Okay, Oklahoma
Boring, Oregon
Intercourse, Pennsylvania
Difficult, Tennessee
Cut and Shoot, Texas
Petty, Texas
Telephone, Texas
Bread Loaf, Vermont
Odd, West Virginia
Sod, West Virginia

Canada
Come-by-Chance,
   Newfoundland
St. Louis de Ha! Ha!, Quebec
Economy, Nova Scotia
Lower Economy, Nova Scotia
Upper Economy, Nova Scotia

Source: http://s88932719.onlinehome.us/townname.htm

Most polluted parks in the U.S.

Many of the national parks in the United States have the dirtiest air in the country, even worse than heavily polluted cities like Los Angeles. The air pollution comes from burning fossil fuels–coal, oil, and gas. The following parks are ranked as the worst:

1. Great Smoky Mountains National Park, Tennessee and North Carolina–ozone pollution rivals that of Los Angeles
2. Shenandoah National Park, Virginia–views from Skyline Drive and the Appalachian Trail shrink to one mile on some summer days thanks to fine-particle pollution
3. Mammoth Cave National Park, Kentucky–ridge top views are among the haziest in the country and, on average, rainfall in the park is ten times more acidic than natural conditions
4. Sequoia and Kings Canyon National Parks, California
5. Acadia National Park, Maine

Stress in the cities, U.S.

Tacoma, Washington, is America's most stressful city, in terms of unemployment, divorce, commuting time, violent and property crime, suicide, alcohol consumption, self-reported "poor mental health," and number of cloudy days. Sperling's, an American firm that prides itself on helping people to find the best place to live, has ranked 100 largest metro areas according to stress levels:

Most stressful cities
Tacoma, Washington–high divorce and unemployment
    rate, lots of cloudy days, but low violent-crime rate
Miami, Florida–highest violent-crime rate, but plenty of
    "positive mental attitude" among residents

New Orleans, Louisiana–high levels of violent crime and
unemployment
Las Vegas, Nevada–highest suicide and divorce rate, but
the greatest number of sunny days
New York, New York–the longest commute for workers,
but low suicide and divorce rates

Least stressful cities
Albany-Schenectady-Troy, New York, and Harrisburg-
Lebanon-Carlisle, Pennsylvania–both areas score well,
despite dreary winters.
Orange Country, California–very low suicide rate
Nassau-Suffolk, New York–lowest violent- and property-
crime rates
Minneapolis-St. Paul, Minnesota–low unemployment
and violent crime, but many cloudy days

Survey of U.S. cities

Amherst, New York, is the safest city in the United States, while Detroit,
Michigan, is the most dangerous, according to publishing and research
company Morgan Quitno Press, which surveyed 322 cities.

Safest	Most dangerous
Amherst, N.Y.	Detroit, Mich.
Mission Viejo, Calif.	Atlanta, Ga.
Brick Township, N.J.	St. Louis, Mo.
Newton, Mass.	Flint, Mich.
Simi Valley, Calif.	Camden, N.J.

Top honeymoon destinations

According to an annual survey carried out by the American magazine *Modern Bride*, the most popular honeymoon destination is Aruba in the Caribbean.

Top 20

1. Aruba
2. Bermuda
3. Florida
4. Hawaii
5. Italy
6. Jamaica
7. Las Vegas
8. Mexico
9. St. Lucia
10. Tahiti
11. U.S. Virgin Islands
12. France
13. British Virgin Islands
14. Fiji
15. Bahamas
16. Dominican Republic
17. England
18. Greece
19. Bali
20. Africa

Top 10 theme parks in the U.S.

In 2002 Florida led the pack when it came to American theme parks, with seven of the nation's Top 10 located in this sunshine state.

Destination	Visitors, in millions
1. The Magic Kingdom, Walt Disney World, Lake Buena Vista, Fla.	14.0
2. Disneyland, Anaheim, Calif.	12.7
3. Epcot, Walt Disney World, Lake Buena Vista, Fla.	8.3
4. Disney-MGM Studios, Walt Disney World, Lake Buena Vista, Fla.	8.0
5. Disney's Animal Kingdom, Walt Disney World, Lake Buena Vista, Fla.	7.3

6. Universal Studios at Universal Orlando, Fla. 6.9
7. Islands of Adventure at Universal Orlando, Fla. 6.1
8. Universal Studios Hollywood,
    Universal City, Calif. 5.2
9. SeaWorld Florida, Orlando, Fla. 5.0
10. Disney's California Adventure, Anaheim, Calif. 4.7

Source: Amusement Business Magazine

Global weather extremes

In 1922 Libya recorded the highest measured temperature ever, with 136°F. On the other end of the scale, Vostok in Antarctica had the lowest measured temperature of -129°F, in 1983.

Highest temperatures

Place	*°F*	*Date*
1. El Azizia, Libya	136	September 13, 1922
2. Death Valley, California	134	July 10, 1913
3. Tirat Tsvi, Israel, SW Asia	129	June 21, 1942
4. Cloncurry, Queensland	128	January 16, 1889
5. Seville, Spain	122	August 4, 1881

Lowest temperatures

1. Vostok, Antarctica	-129	July 21, 1983
2. Oimekon, Russia	-90	February 6, 1933
3. Verkhoyansk, Russia	-90	February 7, 1892
4. Northice, Greenland	-87	January 9, 1954
5. Snag, Yukon, Canada	-81.4	February 3, 1947

Source: National Climatic Data Center

Most destructive earthquakes

The most destructive earthquake ever recorded happened in China in 1556, although some of the worst quakes date back to before 1000 AD.

Date	Location	Deaths
January 23, 1556	China, Shansi	830,000
July 27, 1976	China, Tangshan	255,000
	(= official; estimated: 655,000)	
August 9, 1138	Syria, Aleppo	230,000
May 22, 1927	China, near Xining	200,000
December 22, 856	Iran, Damghan	200,000
December 16, 1920	China, Gansu	200,000
March 23, 893	Iran, Ardabil	150,000
September 1, 1923	Japan, Kwanto	143,000
October 5, 1948	USSR	110,000
December 28, 1908	Italy, Messina	up to 100,000

Source: U.S. Department of the Interior, U.S. Geological Survey

Most visited attractions in the UK

Or, at least, places where heads can be counted and numbers compared– not, of course, that like is being compared with like. There have been some striking differences over the last twenty-five years, as the lists show. As now, back in 1979 places like the British Museum and the Science Museum did not charge for entrance. Since 1979 we have also seen the arrival of new commercially run tourist attractions, such as the Eden Project in Cornwall.

Top 10 attractions, 1979	*Attendance*
1. Tower of London	2,749,000
2. State Apartments, Windsor Castle	820,000
3. Roman Baths & Pump Room, Bath	709,000

4. Stonehenge, Wiltshire	674,000
5. Shakespeare's birthplace, Stratford-upon-Avon	576,000
6. Beaulieu, Hampshire	566,000
7. Hampton Court, London	556,000
8. St. George's Chapel, Windsor	545,000
9. Warwick Castle	467,000
10. Salisbury Cathedral, Wiltshire	450,000

Top 10 attractions, 2003	*Attendance*
1. Blackpool Pleasure Beach	5,737,000
2. British Museum	4,584,000
3. Tate Modern	3,895,746
4. Natural History Museum	2,976,738
5. Science Museum	2,886,859
6. Victoria & Albert Museum	2,257,325
7. Tower of London	1,972,263
8. Eden Project	1,404,737
9. Legoland Windsor	1,321,128
10. National Maritime Museum	1,305,150

Top 5 lawns in the U.S.

New York's Central Park has the nation's best lawn, combining a well-kept turf with the impressive view of the city's skyline. The following is a list of the Top 5 lawns of 2003, according to small engine manufacturer Briggs & Stratton, which produces outdoor power equipment such as lawn mowers:

1. Central Park's Great Lawn–New York, N.Y.
2. Nelson-Atkins Museum of Art–Kansas City, Mo.
3. Piedmont Park–Atlanta, Ga.
4. Minneapolis Sculpture Garden–Minneapolis, Minn.
5. International Peace Garden–Dunseith, N. Dak.

Who invented what

Text messages

Top Internet searches

Computer viruses

It won't work

SCIENCE
AND
TECHNOLOGY

Who invented what

Things are rarely invented just like that, out of the blue, with nothing or no one having gone before, working along a similar path. And very often when the breakthrough comes, it's a team effort. Sometimes no one knows the inventor, the original begetter never having been acknowledged, especially when the invention was a long time ago.

Here are some everyday, domestic objects in constant use, which we all roughly take for granted, with their probable origins.

FIVE INVENTIONS THAT TURN OUT TO BE INCREDIBLY ANCIENT

Glass, 2500 BC: Could have been discovered by accident, when sand got heated with limestone and wood ash. Small glass ornamental beads have been found dating back to 2500 BC, but it was the Egyptians around 1450 BC who developed other uses, such as glass bottles.

Locks, 2000 BC: The Egyptians used a wooden bolt held tight by pins dropped into holes–only a key shaped to push all the pins out of the way could open it. Much like locks today, really.

Socks, 800 BC: The first wearers are not known, but presumably when we gave up bare feet for shoes of some sort, socks of some sort came in. The first mention of them was in a poem by the Greek poet Hesiod around 700 BC. They were bits of felt at first, patched together. Knitted socks were created by the Egyptians around 450 BC.

Metal coins, 600 BC: People often exchanged a piece of precious metal for goods, but there was no standardized exchange value, and it was hard to weigh and evaluate worth. The first known standardized coins, all weighing the same, and stamped with the king's head, were issued around 600 BC by the Lydians in what is now western Turkey.

Central heating, 400 BC: The Romans brought central heating to Britain sometime after 43 AD. You can see roughly how it worked in several bath houses in the Roman Forts on Hadrian's Wall—hot air was conducted along underfloor channels from a central charcoal-burning stove. They called the system "hypocaust," which is Greek, suggesting perhaps the Greeks got there first. Hollow floors have been found in Greek ruins in Turkey.

FIVE REMARKABLY OLDISH INVENTIONS

Spectacles, 1280: A pair of glass lenses, clipped onto the nose, were first noted in the thirteenth century, but no inventor was credited. Spectacle-making was known in Florence from 1301 where Alessandro de Spina and Salvino degli Armatti were credited with inventing them. On the other hand, the Chinese say they got there first around 900 AD.

Watches, 1500: Sundials or shadow clocks used to tell the time date from 3500 BC. The origin of mechanical clocks, fitted into towers, is unknown, but the first striking clock was erected in Milan in 1335. Salisbury Cathedral had one from 1386—it still works. Watches, which could be carried around, were invented by Peter Henlein, a German locksmith, in 1500. The original was about the size of a large mobile phone and was carried by hand.

Pencil, 1565: Invented by Conrad Gesner, a German–Swiss who realized the potential of graphite and encased it in a wooden holder to form a means of writing.

Flush toilet, 1591: John Harrington, an Elizabethan courtier, installed the first recorded one at Richmond Palace.

Umbrella, 1637: Louis XIII of France had one made of oiled cloth, for protection against the sun and rain. The first steel-ribbed opening umbrella was invented by an Englishman, Samuel Fox, in 1874.

EIGHT DEAD-MODERN INVENTIONS

Jeans, 1873: During the Gold Rush in the United States, Levi Strauss Co. supplied prospectors with materials and clothes, including trousers. A tailor named Jacob Davis suggested that trousers made of denim–a material that had originated from Nîmes in France, hence *de Nîmes*–complete with riveted pockets, would go down well. And they did. In 1873 Strauss registered the first patent for jeans.

Toothpaste, 1896: As we know it, coming out of a tube, toothpaste was introduced by William Colgate in 1896. Before that it had been packaged in jars. It was tried in a tube in 1892 by another American, Washington Sheffield, but it didn't quite work. Colgate developed the tube nozzle so that the toothpaste, as it boasted on the side of the tube, "comes out a ribbon, lies flat on the brush."

Safety razor, 1901: Until then, men had shaved with open "cut-throat" blades. King Camp Gillette invented a blade that fitted into a razor and was safe and also disposable, which meant he sold millions. The first electric razor was also invented by an American–Colonel Jacob Schick of the U.S. Army–who wanted to do away with wet shaving.

Brassière, 1914: New York partygoer Mary Jacob didn't like the feel of a whalebone corset under her new slinky dress and so chucked the whalebone and wore some handkerchiefs tied with ribbon over her breasts. In 1914 she patented the brassière, later selling out to a major corset company.

Tupperware, 1946: Another amazing American invention; how would we have survived without it? Earl Tupper designed a plastic box with an airtight seal to be used in fridges–but at first no one was much interested. Then he met ace saleswoman Brownie Wise. She suggested Tupperware parties–where hostesses demonstrated their use, then sold them. The queen, who uses Tupperware at Buckingham Palace, will always be grateful.

Velcro, 1950: The name comes from the French for velvet, "velours," and for hook, "crochet." Swiss inventor George de Mestral noticed how plant burrs clung to his dog, but it took him fifteen years of research to find a way of creating the same effect.

Mobile phone, 1970: Pioneered in the United States by Bell Laboratories, they had a trial run in Chicago in 1979 and opened their first public service in 1983, but meanwhile the Scandinavians had got in first, launching their own system in 1981.

World Wide Web, 1989: Created by English physicist Tim Berners-Lee while working for the European

Centre for Nuclear Research in Switzerland. He needed to get information into computers scattered across the world; he defined the system, wrote the software, then passed it onto the world, for nothing. Thanks, Tim.

Text messages

Almost a third of mobile phone owners use text messaging to arrange their social lives. Many have dumped partners using a text, use it to arrange dates, and to flirt. Others announce their children's birth via text, and/or use it to fire their employees.

According to youth culture researchers Roar, texting meets fundamental emotional and social needs by enabling young people to communicate secretly. It's also practical, affordable, and personalized.

Popular texting

@wrk–at work

A/S–age/sex?

A3–anytime, anywhere, anyplace

AB–ah, bless!

AFAIR–as far as I can remember/recall

Akcdnt–accident

AMBW–all my best wishes

AML–all my love

ASAP–as soon as f****** possible

ATT–about time too

AWCIGO–and where can I get one?

Grr–angry

RTcL–article

RUF2C–are you free to chat?

Top ring tones (Nokia, Sagem, Motorola, and Ericsson phones)
"Swing Low, Sweet Chariot"
"Clocks"–Coldplay
"Where Is the Love?"–Black Eyed Peas
"P.I.M.P."–50 cent featuring Snoop Dogg
"Rhubarb & Custard"
"I Believe in a Thing Called Love"
"Rainbow"
"The Great Escape"
"Harry Potter"–John Williams

Top Internet searches

Top Internet searches in the U.S.

Eight topics have appeared on the Lycos top Internet search list every week since August 1999, ranging from film stars to tattoos.

Pamela Anderson–film and TV star

Dragonball Z–a show about intergalactic warriors

Las Vegas–a popular city to search for, despite a temporary lapse in general searches for tourism and airlines after the September 11 attacks

Jennifer Lopez–singer and film star

Pokémon–Japanese cartoon; the only time it dropped from the Top 20 was the week of September 11

Britney Spears–teen pop star and the number one most searched term of 2000

Tattoos–nearly half of all tattoo requests are incorrectly spelled

WWF–the World Wrestling Federation

Top searches of 2003

KaZaa

Harry Potter

American Idol

Britney Spears

50 Cent

Eminem

WWE (World Wrestling Entertainment)

Paris Hilton

NASCAR

Christina Aguilera

Computer viruses

The first computer virus appeared in 1986, five years after IBM introduced the PC and four years before the birth of the World Wide Web. However, a few years earlier Fred Cohen had already formally defined a computer virus as "a computer program that can affect other computer programs by modifying them in such a way as to include a (possibly evolved) copy of itself."

Newer infections spread faster than ever before, and at its peak the recent MyDoom worm was found in one in nine messages transmitted globally. Here's a list of some of the earliest, most well-known, or most dangerous computer viruses and worms:

1981	Apple 1, 2, and 3	1991	Tequila
1987	Lehigh	1992	The Dark Avenger
1988	Jerusalem		Mutation Engine
	MacMag	1994	Good Times
	Scores	1995	Word Concept

1996	Baza, Laroux, and Staog		Sircam
1998	StrangeBrew		CodeRed
	Chernobyl		BadTrans
1999	Melissa	2002	Shakira
	Bubble Boy		Britney Spears
	Tristate		Jennifer Lopez
2000	The Love Bug		Klez
	The Stages		Bugbear
2001	Nimda	2003	The Slammer
	Anna Kournikova	2004	MyDoom

Source: www.Infoplease.com

It won't work

What they thought at the time. Look at them now . . .

Louis Pasteur's discoveries: "It is absurd to think that germs causing fermentation and putrefaction come from the air; the atmosphere would have to be as thick as pea soup for that." Dr. Nicholas Joly, 1840.

Thomas Edison and electricity: "Do not bother to sell your gas shares. The electric light has no future." Professor John Henry Pepper.

George Stephenson and the opening of the Stockton-Darlington Railway, the world's first: "What can be more palpably absurd and ridiculous than the prospect of locomotives traveling at twice the speed of stagecoaches." *Quarterly Review*, 1825.

Airplanes: "Artificial flight is impossible." Professor Simon Newcomb, director of the U.S. Naval Observatory, 1894.

Alexander Graham Bell and the telephone: "It is impossible to transmit speech electrically. The 'telephone' is as mythical as the unicorn." Professor Poggendorf, 1860.

Television: "I showed them my invention for television. They evinced polite curiosity and then informed me that they were convinced that the transmission of images–especially mentioning fog as an impediment–was impossible." John Logie Baird in a letter, 1940.

Space travel: "In a sense, interplanetary travel is and remains utter bilge; the difficulties of setting up a launching station to arrange a safe return are enormous." Dr. Richard Woolley, Astronomer Royal, 1960.

The law and lawyers

Odd laws

Bizarre accidents in the UK

Americans' biggest worries

The UK's biggest worries

What we don't know

UFO sightings in North America

SOCIETY

The law and lawyers

"The law is an ass," said Mr. Bumble in *Oliver Twist*. That was in fiction, but in real life Charles Dickens and many other worthies have had equally uncomplimentary things to say about our legal friends.

The Bible: "Woe unto you lawyers, for you have taken away the key of knowledge." Luke 11:52.

Cicero: "The more laws, the less justice."

Shakespeare: "The first thing we do, let's kill all the lawyers." *Henry VI, Part II.*

Jonathan Swift: "Laws are like cobwebs, which may catch small flies, but let wasps and hornets break through."

Oliver Goldsmith: "Laws grind the poor and rich men rule the law."

Charles Dickens: "The great principle of the English law is to make business for itself."

Thomas Jefferson: "It is the trade of lawyers to question everything, yield nothing, and talk by the hour."

Franz Kafka: "A lawyer is a person who writes a 10,000-word document and calls it a brief."

Pierre Joseph Proudhon: "Laws: we know what they are, and what they are worth. They are spiderwebs for the rich and mighty, steel chains for the poor and weak, fishing nets in the hand of the government."

J. P. Morgan: "I don't want a lawyer to tell me what I cannot do; I hire him to tell me how to do what I want to do."

John Keats: "I think we may class the lawyer in the natural history of monsters."

Clarence Darrow: "The law does not pretend to punish everything that is dishonest. That would seriously interfere with business."

John Mortimer: "No brilliance is required in law, just common sense and relatively clean fingernails."

Odd laws

If you've ever moved rhythmically to music in a premises with a liquor license then you've broken the law–according to the Licensing Act of 1964. And according to a law passed in 1845, attempting to commit suicide was a capital offense. Offenders could be hanged for trying. Those laws applied to England, but here's a list of equally strange laws around the world:

Glasgow: It is illegal to be drunk and in possession of a cow

Bangkok: It is illegal to leave your house not wearing underwear

Victoria, Australia: Drivers can be fined for resting an arm out of the car window

Halifax, Canada: Wearing scented body products is banned

Athens, Greece: A driver's license can be suspended if the driver is deemed either "poorly dressed" or "unbathed"

Quebec, Canada: Legally, margarine must be a different color from butter

France: It is illegal to sell dolls that do not have human faces

Alabama: It's illegal to wear a fake mustache that causes laughter in church

Fairbanks, Alaska: It is illegal to feed alcoholic beverages to a moose

San Francisco, California: It is illegal to wipe one's car with used underwear

Pueblo, Colorado: It is illegal to let a dandelion grow within city limits

Hartford, Connecticut: It is illegal to educate a dog

Florida: Unmarried women who parachute on Sundays may be jailed

Chicago, Illinois: It is illegal to fish in one's pajamas

Massachusetts: It is illegal to duel with water pistols

Minnesota: Women can face up to thirty days in jail if they impersonate Santa Claus

Nebraska: It is illegal for a mother to give her daughter a perm without a state license

Waterloo, Nebraska: Barbers are forbidden from eating onions between 7 a.m. and 7 p.m.

New Jersey: It is illegal to "frown" at a police officer

Youngstown, Ohio: It is illegal to run out of gas

Salt Lake City, Utah: It is illegal to carry an unwrapped ukulele on the street

Vermont: It is illegal to deny the existence of God

IN NEW YORK ALL THE FOLLOWING ARE ILLEGAL:

Smoking in public

Drinking alcohol in public

Feeding pigeons

Riding a bike with your feet off the pedals

Using mobile phones in cinemas

Ashtrays (except in private homes)

Variety of web and print sources, inc: www.members.tripod.com

Bizarre accidents in the UK

Nearly a million people a year end up in the hospital after suffering bizarre accidents, estimated to cost around £1billion a year for treatment. Here are just some of them:

Contact with a nonpowered hand-drill	3,038
Incidents with lawn mowers	369
Contact with plant thorns, spines, sharp leaves	190
Bitten or crushed by reptiles	51
Bitten by a rat	22

Source: Department of Health

Americans' biggest worries

Despite fears of terrorist attacks, Americans remain most anxious about finances and the death of loved ones, according to the Anxiety Disorders Association of America.

36% of people are "very" or "extremely" worried about their financial status

31% are anxious about a loved one dying

10% worry about their own death

Almost 50% have avoided people when feeling worried or anxious

Two in five have avoided answering their phones

For one in seven people, their worries have prevented them from leaving their homes

The UK's Biggest worries

Londoners are the biggest worriers in the UK, repeatedly losing sleep over the well-being of family members and hospital waiting lists. Concern about personal health and fitness also rates high on the list, as does the cost of living.

PERCENTAGE OF ADULTS WORRIED ABOUT:

Issue	London	UK
Family well-being	84	72
State of health service	82	80
Cost of living	82	70
Personal level of health/fitness	80	59
Way government runs the country	74	73
Financial well-being	74	73
Job satisfaction	73	52
Standard of living	72	48
State of British economy	72	63
Threat of terrorism	70	61
Neighborhood crime	70	55
Local traffic	69	48
Immediate surroundings	69	48
Contact with family/friends	67	50
Personal stress levels	66	48
Local education facilities	64	44
Job security	64	51
Work/life balance	64	49
Saving the environment	61	66
Investment climate, Britain	53	40
Level of noise where you live	52	30
Journey to work	48	26

Source: JPMorgan Fleming survey

What we don't know

Almost half of the British population has no idea who the deputy prime minister is, while many are convinced United Nations Secretary General Kofi Annan is an Iraqi general.

Don't know deputy prime minister	47%
Embarrassed about general knowledge	12%

Source: study carried out for Whitaker's Almanack

UFO sightings in North America

One of the most commonly shaped UFOs reported to America's National UFO Reporting Center is a triangle, followed by a disk. But hardly anyone has sighted a dome or a pyramid.

The center is located in Seattle, Washington, and was founded in 1974. It has a collection of UFO sightings dating as far back as 1860. The center's Web site has this disclaimer: "The National UFO Reporting Center makes no claims as to the validity of the information in any of these reports. Obvious hoaxes have been omitted."

The following is a list of some of the shapes reported over the years.

Shape	Number reported
Cigar	705
Circle	1,945
Cone	121
Crescent	2
Cross	73
Cylinder	419
Diamond	401
Disk	2,115
Dome	1
Egg	327

Fireball	1,600
Flare	1
Flash	385
Hexagon	1
Light	4,756
Oval	1,073
Pyramid	1
Rectangle	351
Round	2
Sphere	1,387
Teardrop	238
Triangle	2,403

Your best chance of sighting an UFO in North America is in Washington or Texas. The list below shows the states and provinces with the highest number of reportings.

State	Sightings reported
Arizona	909
British Columbia, Can.	443
California	3,191
Colorado	521
Florida	1,019
Georgia	355
Illinois	729
Indiana	371
Massachusetts	360
Michigan	632
Missouri	500
North Carolina	428
New Jersey	427
Nevada	356
New York	984
Ohio	725
Ontario, Can.	495

Oregon	724
Pennsylvania	676
Tennessee	353
Texas	1,122
Virginia	385
Washington	1,770
Wisconsin	447

TRANSPORT AND TRAVEL

Excuses for train delays

The most popular excuse for a late train in the UK is the weather–be it snow, ice, leaves, wind, or heat. Another common justification is the presence of something–or someone–on the line.

Here's an A to Z of less common excuses given for delays:

A drunk man on the line
Delayed due to the Royal Escort–
 the Royals can't be held up at
 any level crossing so the trains
 get delayed instead
Deranged female on the line
Driver abandons train
Driver having his tea break
Driver held up in freeway traffic
Due to no reason whatsoever
Exploding pigeon
Guard arrested for excess ticket
 fraud and taken away by police
Herons mating
Horse on the line
Overhanging tree branches
Person by the side of the line
 with a rifle

Portakabin (a portable storage
 unit) blocking the line
Rat self-destructed while
 chewing through signaling
 cables
Rugby-related problems
Slippery rails all over the country
Some fool's used an alarm handle
 as a coat hook
The f****** train's broken down
Train delayed due to Madonna
 (Liverpool Street, 1995 when
 Great Eastern held the last train
 of the evening to allow concert-
 goers to return from Wembley)
Trainspotters on the line

Source: www.rodge.force9.co.uk

Subway delays

If you've been stuck on a subway when the train suddenly stops–or been left standing waiting on a platform for a subway that never comes–then sometimes it's reassuring to be told the reason why, and sometimes not . . .

Subway announcements

"Ladies and gentlemen, I do apologize for the delay to your service. I know you're all dying to get home, unless, of course, you happen to be married to my ex-wife, in which case you'll want to cross over to the westbound and go in the opposite direction."

"Your delay this evening is caused by the line controller suffering from E & B syndrome, not knowing his elbow from his backside. I'll let you know any further information as soon as I'm given any."

"Do you want the good news first or the bad news? The good news is that last Friday was my birthday and I hit the town and had a great time. The bad news is that there is a points failure somewhere between Stratford and East Ham, which means we probably won't reach our destination."

"Ladies and gentlemen, we apologize for the delay, but there is a security alert at Victoria station and we are therefore stuck here for the foreseeable future, so let's take our minds off it and pass some time together. All together now . . . 'Ten green bottles, hanging on a wall . . .' "

"We are now traveling through Baker Street; as you can see Baker Street is closed. It would have been nice if they had actually told me, so I could tell you earlier, but no, they don't think about things like that."

"Beggars are operating on this train. Please do *not* encourage these professional beggars. If you have any spare change, please give it to a registered charity. Failing that, give it to me."
"Let the passengers off the train *first*! [pause . . .] Oh go on then, stuff yourselves in like sardines, see if I care–I'm going home."

"Please allow the doors to close. Try not to confuse this with 'Please hold the doors open.' The two are distinct and separate instructions."

"Please note that the beeping noise coming from the doors means that the doors are about to close. It does not mean throw yourself or your bags into the doors."

"We can't move off because some idiot has their effing hand stuck in the door."

"To the gentleman wearing the long gray coat trying to get on the second carriage—what part of 'stand clear of the doors' don't you understand?"

"Please move all baggage away from the doors. [pause . . .] Please move *all* belongings away from the doors. [pause . . .] This is a personal message to the man in the brown suit wearing glasses at the rear of the train—put the pie down, four-eyes, and move your bloody golf clubs away from the door before I come down there and shove them up your a** sideways."

"May I remind all passengers that there is strictly no smoking allowed on any part of the underground. However, if you are smoking a joint, it's only fair that you pass it round the rest of the carriage."

Source: Skiver's Corner, *BBC Lancashire*

Top-selling vehicles in the U.S.

The most popular vehicle with American buyers is the full-size pickup truck. The following are the best-sellers for 2003:

Ford F-Series
Chevrolet Silverado
Dodge Ram

Toyota Camry
Honda Accord

Source: J. D. Power and Associates

North America's favorite car colors

Silver was North America's most popular car color for 2003, according to DuPont Automotive. The following list shows the color of cars produced in the United States and Canada in 2003; the numbers are said to provide a good indication of actual popularity.

Color	Percentage of cars
Silver	20.2
White	18.4
Black	11.6
Medium/Dark gray	11.5
Light brown	8.8

Most stolen cars in the U.S.

There were 1.2 million motor vehicle thefts in the United States in 2002, according to the National Insurance Crime Bureau. Its figures include cars that have parts removed or are taken for joyrides and later recovered.

Top 5 models for 2002
Toyota Camry
Honda Accord
Honda Civic
Chevrolet Full-Size Pickup
Ford Full-Size Pickup

Most stolen color
White
Red
Blue
Black
Green

Source: MSN Autos

Shady insurance claims

Ever had an accident in the car that just *wasn't your fault*? So have these people . . . the following are said to be actual statements found on insurance claim forms where car drivers tried to sum up what happened to them:

"I told the police that I was not injured, but on removing my hat I found that I had a fractured skull."

"I pulled away from the side of the road, glanced at my mother-in-law and headed over the embankment."

"I thought my window was down, but I found it was up when I put my head through it."

"I collided with a stationary truck coming the other way."

"Coming home I drove into the wrong house and collided with a tree I don't have. The other car collided with mine without giving me warning of its intention."

"A pedestrian hit me and went under my car."

"The guy was all over the road. I had to swerve several times before I hit him."

"In an attempt to kill a fly, I drove into a telephone pole."

"I had been shopping for a plant all day and was on my way home. As I reached an intersection a hedge sprang up, obscuring my vision, and I did not see the other car."

"I was on the way to the doctor with rear-end trouble when my universal joint gave way causing me to have an accident and damage my big end."

"I had been driving for forty years when I fell asleep at the wheel and had an accident."

"As I approached the intersection a sign appeared in a place where no stop sign had ever appeared before. I was unable to stop in time to avoid the accident."

"To avoid hitting the bumper of the car in front I struck a pedestrian."

"My car was legally parked as it backed into another vehicle."

"An invisible car came out of nowhere, struck my car, and vanished."

"I was sure the old fellow would never make it to the other side of the road when I struck him."

"The telephone pole was approaching. I was attempting to swerve out the way when I struck the front end."

"I saw a slow-moving, sad-faced old gentleman as he bounced off the roof of my car."

"The indirect cause of the accident was a little guy in a small car with a big mouth."

"The pedestrian had no idea which direction to run. So I ran over him."

"I was thrown from my car as it left the road. I was later found in a ditch by some stray cows."

"The accident was caused by me waving to the man I hit last week."

"I knocked over a man; he admitted it was his fault as he'd been knocked over before."

The finest hotels in the world

The following list comprises the hotels that *Tatler* magazine considers the finest in the world. It compiled a shortlist of fifteen hotels for its 2003 Hotel of the Year *Tatler* Travel Awards.

Hotel	Cost
Chateau de Bagnols, Beaujolais	£300 to £840 per room per night
North Island, Seychelles	seven nights from £3,150 inc. flight
Oberoi, Mauritius	£350 to £500 per room per night
One Aldwych, London	£300 to £1000 per room per night
One & Only Le Touessrok, Mauritius	£400 to £500 per person per night
Barnsley House, Gloucestershire	£250 to £450 per room
Kurland, Plettenberg Bay, South Africa	from £140 per person per night
Elounda Gulf Villas, Crete	£105 to £1980 per room
Four Seasons, New York, N.Y. and Beverly Hills	from $319 per person per night
Hotel Tresanton, St. Mawes, Cornwall	£165 to £265 per room
The Standard, Downtown LA	£72 to £289 per person per night
Soho House, New York, N.Y.	$250 to $795 per room
Singita, Lebombo, South Africa	R6,625 per person per night
Taha'a Pearl beach, Tahiti	£380 to £520 per person per night
Vanyavilas, Rajasthan, India	£275 per person per night

Hotel notices

Ever seen a strange notice–in even stranger English–in a hotel room abroad? Here's a list of helpful tips found in European hotels:

DO NOT ENTER THE LIFT BACKWARDS,
AND ONLY WHEN LIT UP
(German hotel)

TO MOVE THE CABIN, PUSH BUTTON FOR WISHING
FLOOR. IF THE CABIN SHOULD ENTER MORE PERSONS,
EACH ONE SHOULD PRESS A NUMBER OF WISHING
FLOOR DRIVING IS THEN GOING ALPHABETICALLY BY
NATIONAL ORDER
(elevator in Belgrade hotel)

THE FLATTENING OF UNDERWEAR WITH PLEASURE IS
THE JOB OF THE CHAMBERMAID
(Yugoslavian hotel)

NOT TO PERAMBULATE THE CORRIDORS IN THE HOURS
OF REPOSE IN THE BOOTS OF ASCENSION
(Austrian hotel)

IN CASE OF FIRE, DO YOUR UTMOST TO ALARM THE
HOTEL PORTER
(Vienna hotel)

LADIES ARE REQUESTED
NOT TO HAVE CHILDREN IN THE BAR
(Norwegian hotel)

THIS HOTEL IS RENOWNED FOR ITS PEACE AND
SOLITUDE. IN FACT, CROWDS FROM ALL OVER THE
WORLD FLOCK HERE TO ENJOY ITS SOLITUDE
(Italian hotel brochure)

AND IN JAPAN:
GUESTS ARE REQUESTED NOT TO SMOKE
OR DO OTHER DISGUSTING BEHAVIORS IN BED
(Tokyo hotel)

IS FORBIDDEN TO STEAL HOTEL TOWELS.
PLEASE IF YOU ARE NOT A PERSON TO DO SUCH A THING
IS PLEASE NOT TO READ NOTICE
(another Tokyo hotel)

COOLS AND HEATS: IF YOU WANT JUST CONDITION OF
WARM AIR IN YOUR ROOM, PLEASE CONTROL YOURSELF
(information booklet, Japanese hotel)

AS FOR SHOP AND OFFICE NOTICES:
LADIES HAVE FITS UPSTAIRS
(dress shop, Hong Kong)

ORDER YOUR SUMMERS SUIT BECAUSE IS BIG RUSH,
WE WILL EXECUTE CUSTOMERS IN STRICT ROTATION
(tailor shop, Rhodes)

LADIES, LEAVE YOUR CLOTHES HERE AND SPEND
THE AFTERNOON HAVING A GOOD TIME
(laundry in Rome)

FUR COATS MADE FOR LADIES
FROM THEIR OWN SKIN
(furrier in Sweden)

SPECIALIST IN WOMEN AND OTHER DISEASES
(doctor's office, Rome)

Source: variety of Web sites

Travel tips

The following list is taken from travel Web sites that provide crucial
tips for those traveling abroad:

Bangkok–go upstairs to
Departures upon your arrival
where you can get a cheaper taxi
fare into the city

Jamaica–do not buy marijuana
from anybody at the Kingston
port or airport

Orlando–choose the left-hand line at Orlando theme parks, it will be shorter. Americans drive on the right-hand side of the road and they all go for the right-hand line

Planes–the best economy seat on a 747 is the last one: there are only two seats in a three-seat area, it's close to the loos, you get fed and watered first

Russia–if you're traveling there in the summer, take plenty of mosquito spray

Safari–when camping or going on safari take a toilet roll with a string tied through the middle. This can be hung round your neck when visiting the toilets, making it easily accessible and not likely to be dropped on wet/dirty floors

Singapore –take a small solar-powered calculator with you when you go shopping

Sri Lanka–please and thank you are not common words, it's done with a smile

South Africa–lock your car doors at all times because of car-hijacking

What to do–and not do–in Japan
Take your shoes off if you go into a Japanese house and leave them on the step outside.
Take slip-on shoes, they are easier to get off than laces.
Don't sit on a table.
Don't put your shoes on a table or chair, even in the train.
If you have to stand on a chair, take your shoes off first.
If you have a problem with sweaty feet, use a foot deodorant.
Don't hug or kiss.
Don't call anyone by their first name.

Quotations on the United States

Things you were told as a child ...

Things your parents said to you ...

How to make your own luck

How to make people like you

Boy or girl? Predicting baby gender

Packing your labor bag for the hospital

Good reasons not to get divorced

Things not to do during an interview

What not to say

What not to say to a Canadian abroad

WISDOM
AND
ADVICE

Quotations on the United States

America's really only a kind of Russia.
ANTHONY BURGESS, *Honey for Bears*

The business of America is business.
CALVIN COOLIDGE, 1925 speech

Whatever America hopes to bring to pass in this world
must first come to pass in the heart of America.
PRESIDENT EISENHOWER, 1953 inaugural address

Dearest Alice, I could come back to America
(could be carried back on a stretcher) to die–
but never, never to live.
HENRY JAMES, in a letter to his sister-in-law Alice James

In the United States there is more space where nobody
is than where anybody is. That is what makes
America what it is.
GERTRUDE STEIN, *The Geographical History of America*

Source: The Penguin Dictionary of Modern Quotations

Things you were told as a child and believed at the time

If the wind changes your face will stick like that.

If you eat carrots you'll be able to see in the dark.

Eat your crusts, it'll make your hair curly.

You'll catch cold if you go out with wet hair.

Eating spinach will make you strong.

If you swallow chewing gum, it'll stick your insides together.

If you sit on a stone step you'll get a chill in your kidneys.

If you squeeze it, it'll never get better.

That'll put hairs on your chest.

If you eat the seeds out of an apple you will get an apple tree growing from your tummy and out your ears.

If you fiddle with your belly button, your butt will unscrew.

Chewing gum is made of horse's hooves.

If you pick your nose, your head will cave in.

Things your parents said to you that you swore you'd never say to your own kids, but do . . .

Of course it won't hurt.

Because I said so!

Wait 'til your dad gets home!

We never had PlayStations/mobile phones/shoes when we were young.

Eat your broccoli.

I never did that when I was your age.

You don't know you're born.

No.

I remember when . . .

Haven't you grown?

Take your coat off so you'll feel the benefit of it when you go outside again.

You'll poke someone's eye out with that!

If you get run over I'll kill you.

Do you want a smack?

D'ya think I'm made o' money?

You'll laugh on the other side of your face in a minute!

Do you think money grows on trees?

You'd look after it/them if you had to pay for it/them.

Don't look down the drain, 'cause you'll get scarlet fever.

If you pick at a zit it'll grow into a pig's foot.

You're not going out looking like that!

Put your coat on, you'll catch your death.

Wait till you have kids of your own

Make sure you've got clean underwear on, in case you get run over.

That's not music—it's just noise!

When I was your age…

How to make your own luck

Most people know it's lucky to find a four-leaf clover— but what about lucky elephant pictures?

A list of things to bring good luck

A horseshoe, hung above the doorway, will bring good luck to a home (some believe the horseshoe should be facing downward, others that it must be turned upward).

An acorn should be carried to bring luck and ensure a long life.

Spit on a new baseball bat before using it for the first time to make it lucky.

If a black cat walks towards you, it brings good fortune (but if it walks away, it takes the good luck with it).

Pictures of an elephant bring luck, but only if they face a door.

**A list of things
that could bring bad luck**
Seeing an ambulance is very
unlucky unless you pinch your
nose or hold your breath until
you see a black or a brown dog.

It's bad luck to put a hat on a bed.

Placing a bed facing north and
south brings misfortune.

You must get out of bed on the
same side that you get in or you
will have bad luck.

If a bee enters your home, it's a
sign that you will soon have a
visitor. If you kill the bee, you
will have bad luck, or the visitor
will be unpleasant.

To drop a comb while you are
combing your hair is a sign of a
coming disappointment.

It's bad luck to leave a house
through a different door than the
one used to come into it.

It's bad luck to say the word "pig"
while fishing at sea.

To break a mirror means seven
years bad luck.

It's bad luck to close a pocket-
knife unless you were the one
who opened it.

It's bad luck to let milk boil over.

Bad luck will follow the spilling
of salt unless a pinch is thrown
over the left shoulder into the
face of the devil waiting there.

Do not place shoes upon a table,
for this will bring bad luck for
the day, cause trouble with your
mate, and you might even lose
your job as a result.

Sparrows carry the souls of the
dead; it's unlucky to kill one.

It's bad luck to open an umbrella
inside the house, especially if you
put it over your head.

**A list of things
not to do on a Friday**
A bed changed on Friday will
bring bad dreams.

Any ship that sails on Friday will
have bad luck.

You should never start a trip on
Friday or you will meet
misfortune.

It is bad luck to cut your fingernails on Friday.

Never start to make a garment on Friday unless you can finish it the same day.

Source:www.corsinet.com

How to make people like you

Dale Carnegie, author of the 1930s blockbuster *How to Win Friends and Influence People*, devised this list in order to help people make friends.

Six ways to make people like you
Rule 1: Become genuinely interested in other people.
Rule 2: Smile.
Rule 3: Remember that a man's name is to him the sweetest and most important sound in the English language.
Rule 4: Be a good listener. Encourage others to talk about themselves.
Rule 5: Talk in terms of the other man's interest.
Rule 6: Make the other person feel important–and do it sincerely.

And he compiled this helpful list for improving your home life:

Seven rules for making your home life happier
Rule 1: Don't nag.
Rule 2: Don't try to make your partner over.
Rule 3: Don't criticize.
Rule 4: Give honest appreciation.
Rule 5: Pay little attentions.
Rule 6: Be courteous.
Rule 7: Read a good book on the sexual side of marriage.

Boy or girl? Predicting baby gender

Anyone who has been pregnant knows how much other people like guessing the sex of your unborn child. While modern tests like ultrasound and amniocentesis can spot the gender, here's a list of more traditional ways of playing the guessing game.

The following means it will be a boy
You carry high
The bump is all out at the front
The baby's heart rate is slow
The hair on your legs is growing faster during pregnancy
You are sleeping in a bed with your pillow to the north
Your feet are colder than they were before pregnancy
The father-to-be is gaining weight as well
The maternal grandmother has grey hair
Your urine is bright yellow
Your nose has been spreading
You have been craving meats or cheeses
You are looking particularly attractive during pregnancy
Your belly gets hairy
Your hands are dry and chapped

And these mean it will be a girl
You carry low
The bump is wide
Bad morning sickness
The baby's heart rate is fast (140 or more beats per minute)
You refuse to eat the crust of a loaf of bread
You had morning sickness early in pregnancy
Your breasts are dramatically increased during pregnancy
You are craving sweets
You get red highlights in your hair

Other ways for mothers-to-be to tell
Pick up a key. If you pick it up by the round end, it will be a

boy. If you pick it up by the long end, it will be a girl. And if you pick it up in the middle, you'll be having twins.

Hang a gold pendant over the palm of your hand. If the pendant moves in a circular fashion, it will be a girl. If it swings back and forth, it will be a boy.

The same goes for hanging a needle (or a wedding band) on a thread over your belly.

What side do you lie on while resting? On your left, it's boy, on your right, it's a girl.

Ask the mom-to-be to show her hands. If she shows them palm up it's a boy, palms down and it's a girl.

Various sources, including www.babycentre.co.uk,
www.yourbaby.co.uk, www.smilechild.co.uk

Packing your labor bag for the hospital

Pregnant women are advised to pack a bag with all the essentials towards the last two weeks of pregnancy in order to get ready for their hospital stay. BBC parenting advisers offer the following list of what to take with you for labor:

A clean T-shirt or front-opening nighties, dressing gown, and slippers–plus socks if you have a tendency to get cold feet

Maternity pads–nighttime sanitary pads are fine–and underpants

Drinks and snacks for you and whoever is going to be with you

A small facial sponge, for dabbing and sucking on

Body oil, fine talcum powder, or lotion for back rubs

Music tapes/CDs and a battery-operated player

A hairband and brush, soap towel and flannel, toothbrush and paste, other toiletries as desired

Other experts offer a more comprehensive list, including the following:
Your birth plan

TENS machine plus spare batteries

Aromatherapy oils to scent the room

A fine water spray for cooling your face

Chapstick

A thermos of ice cubes to suck on

Hot-water bottle

Slippers, in case you're pacing the corridors trying to encourage progress in a slow labor

Spare shirt or T-shirt for your partner, it can be extremely hot in the hospital. He may even want to change into shorts

Bathing trunks for your labor partner if he is planning to physically support you in a birthing pool

Special object to help you focus during labor

Notebook in which to write a record of the labor–and a pen

Camera

Change or phone card for letting relatives and friends know the news

Various sources, including www.babyworld.co.uk

Good reasons not to get divorced

The most common reasons for divorce are abuse and infidelity. But one relationship expert has come up with a list of the 10 most common reasons why people don't get divorced.

1. Loving one's spouse despite the spouse's serious shortcomings

2. Personal values–a staunch belief in the sanctity of marriage

3. Religious convictions

4. Limited financial resources or complex family financial entanglements

5. Worry that additional emotional damage will be inflicted on oneself, children and/or extended family

6. Fear of being a one-, two-, or three-time divorce loser

7. Inconvenience of dismantling hearth and home

8. Poor health and lack of physical and emotional stamina

9. Fear of living alone

10. Ashamed of being considered a failure

Source: "Should I Stay or Go? How Controlled Separation Can Save Your Marriage," *quoted on www.leeraffel.com*

Things not to do during an interview

The following list is provided by career's advice services in order to help interviewees.

1. Do not arrive late. You must allow enough time from when you leave your house to permit for unforeseen circumstances such as rail problems or traffic jams.

2. Do not fidget with items on the desk, or play with your hair and clothes.

3. Do not mumble, talk too fast, too softly, or nonstop. Unless you speak clearly all of your sound comments will be lost on the interviewer and you will not impress.

4. Do not use slang words, crack silly jokes, or chew gum.

5. Do not lean on the interviewer's desk or frequently glance at your watch.

6. Do not hide any aspect of your previous record, overstate qualifications, brag, or get angry.

7. Do not call the interviewer by his/her first name, or become involved in any negative aspect of your current employer, classes, or university.

8. Do not show ignorance about the company–allow your research to come through in conversation.

9. Do not appear half-asleep; go to bed early the night before the interview and sleep soundly knowing that you are fully prepared for the day ahead.

10. Do not bring up the topic of salary. When the time is right, salary will be discussed.

11. If it is an interview over lunch, do not order the spaghetti.

12. Do not come across as being passive or indifferent, be positive and enthusiastic.

13. Do not be overbearing or conceited.

14. Be friendly and open, but do not flirt with the interviewer.

15. Do not use negative body language, or convey inappropriate aspects of your character.

Most importantly:
16. Do not ask to see the interviewer's résumé to see if they are qualified to judge you as a candidate.

17. Do not overemphasize your ability to use a photocopier.

18. Do not, upon walking into the office for the first time, ask the receptionist to hold all your calls.

19. Do not explain that your long-term goal is to have the interviewer's job.

What not to say

What not to say to a police officer when you get pulled over:
I can't reach my license unless you hold my beer.

Sorry, officer, I didn't realize my radar detector wasn't plugged in.

Aren't you the guy from the Village People?

Hey, you must have been doing about 125mph to keep up with me! Well done!

I thought you had to be in relatively good physical condition to be a police officer?

What not to say to a reporter:
This is off the record–the reporter will now carefully note everything you say and reproduce it, to your acute embarrassment.

I've never heard of your magazine/radio show/TV program–local reporters grow up to be national reporters so treat them well.

This afternoon? Don't be ridiculous, we're not working to your deadlines–the media is driven by deadlines, this is a good way to guarantee no publicity or bad publicity.

No comment–you will then be quoted as declining to confirm or deny rumors, or you'll be described as refusing point-blank to talk.

I think I could let you have one of these free (wink)–don't try to buy publicity with bribes, it could backfire.

Source: Mediacoach Web site

What not to say to a Canadian abroad

The following list was compiled by www.thecanadapage.org as some of the most annoyingly frequent statements made to Canadians living abroad.

So . . . it's like cold there, right?

Who is your president?

You're from Canada. Do you know [so and so] from [random Canadian city]?

Aren't you guys British?

Do you like Bryan Adams?

Hey! I saw [random Canadian actor/singer] on TV yesterday! And he's Canadian–I was going to call you.

Can you say aboot for me? Eh?

So when are you guys going to join the U.S.?

WORDS

Hard words

The *Oxford Dictionary of Synonyms and Antonyms* has, at the end of the book, eighty-five pages of what they call "A lexicon of Hard Words." Just in case at this very moment you should be playing Scrabble, and are desperate for a word beginning with A or perhaps Z, to confound your opponent, here are the first five and last five in their invaluable lexicon.

A

aam–a former liquid wine measure of 37-41 gallons; a cask

abatia (also **abattis**)–a defense made of felled trees with the boughs pointing outward

abecedarian–1) one occupied in learning the alphabet 2) a teacher of the alphabet

aberdevine–a bird-fancier's name for the siskin, a small bird like a goldfinch

aberrant–diverging from the normal type or accepted standard

Z

ziggurat–a rectangular stepped tower in ancient Mesopotamia, with a temple on top

zillah–an administrative district in India

zoetrope–an old-fashioned optical toy in the form of a picture-lined cylinder producing moving images when revolved and viewed through a slit

zymosis–fermentation

zymurgy–the branch of applied chemistry dealing with the use of fermentation in brewing, etc.

Top 10 words of 2003 in the U.S.

Your.Dictionary.com has compiled lists of the top words, phrases, and slang of 2003. The lists feature words that made the news in the United States last year, with many originating from the war in Iraq.

Top 10 words
Embedded
Blog
SARS
Spam
Taikonaut
Bushism
Allision
Recall
Middangeard
Celibacy

Top 10 slang terms
What up?
Give it up!
Shut up!
Stog (cigarette)
SNAG (Sensitive New Age
   Guy)
Hottie

Poppins (meaning "perfect")
Tricked Out (suped-up)
Rice Rockets (tricked-out
   Japanese compact cars)
Side Show (temporarily
   cordoning off a freeway to
   perform car stunts in
   tricked-out rice rockets)

Top 10 phrases
Shock-and-Awe
Rush to War
Tire Pressure
Weapons of Mass Destruction
16 Words
Guantanamo Bay
Spider-Hole
Tipping Point
Angry Left
Halliburton Energy Services

Acronyms

Many of the acronyms below originated from the 1980s, when they were popular terms used in marketing or advertising, except for TIRED, which is a twenty-first-century invention.

Tired: Thirtysomething Independent Radical Educated Dropout

Yuppies: Young Urban Professionals

Yummies: Young Urban Mothers

Dinkies: Double Income No Kids

Sinkies: Single Income No Kids

Sitcom: Single Income Two Children Oppressive Marriage

Minkie: Middle Income No Kids

Poupie: Porsche-Owning Urban Professional

Swell: Single Woman Earning Lots of Loot (Miss Yuppie)

Guppies: Greenpeace Yuppies

Bobo: Burnt Out But Opulent

Empty Nesters: Couples whose children are grown up and away

Woopie: Well Off Older People

Jollies: Jet-Setting Oldsters with Lots of Loot

Glams: Greying Leisured Affluent Middle-Aged

Deccie: D.I.Y. Decorators Who Drag, Stipple, and Marble

Splappie: Stripped Pine Laura Ashley People

Drabbie: Ethical urban quaker with anti and pro views

Dockney: East Docklands London Yuppie

Tweenie: Between five and twelve years old

Ladettes: Young women who act like loutish lads

Grey Panthers: Senior citizens with opinion

You say tomatoes . . .

Americans and Brits may speak the same English language–but what we call one thing, they call another. Here's a list:

U.S.	UK
candy	sweets
eggplant	aubergine
sandwich roll	bap
cookie	biscuit
(wild) black raspberry	bramble
pastries	cakes
cotton candy	candy floss
cornstarch	cornflour
zucchini	courgette
potato chips	crisps
French fries	chips
popsicles	iced lollies/lollipops
baked potato	jacket potato
gelatin (Jell-O)	jelly
okra (also bhindi)	ladyfingers
snow peas	mange-tout
granola	muesli
liquor store	off-license/offie
golden raisins	sultana
rutabaga	swede
whole wheat	wholemeal

American mountain biking slang

You're wearing your brain bucket and you're nicely dialed in, when you suddenly have a close encounter with a banana scraper and end up bonked and about to honk. Which sport are you enjoying?

Slang terms used in mountain biking often come from the off-road motorcycling culture, while many of the terms for "crash" came from skiing, snowboarding, surfing, or skating. The following is a selection of slang terms taken from the online slang dictionary.

acro-brat *n.* little kids who use their bikes like pogo sticks, with pegs coming out of the front axle

bacon *n.* scabs on a rider's knees, elbows, or other body parts

bag *v.* to fail to show. "Tom swore he'd be there but he bagged"

banana scraper *n.* low-hanging branches

biff *n.* a crash

bonk *v.* to run out of energy or grow exhausted on a ride. "I bonked so early it was embarrassing"

brain bucket *n.* helmet

brain sieve *n.* a helmet featuring more vents than protective surface

bring home a Christmas tree *v.* to ride (or crash) through dense bushes, so leaves and branches are hanging from your bike and helmet

chi-chi *n.* extravagant parts used to dress up a bicycle to make it more impressive looking

clotheslined *v.* the act of catching an upper body part (*e.g.* the neck) on a low piece of vegetation, resulting in separation of the rider from the bike

death cookies *n.* fist-sized rocks that knock your bike in every direction but the one you want to proceed in

dialed in *adj.* when a bike is set up nicely and everything works just right

endo *n.* the maneuver of flying unexpectedly over the handlebars, thus being forcibly ejected from the bike. Short for "end over end"

gonzo *adj.* treacherous, extreme. "That vertical drop was sheer gonzo"

gnarl *n.* extreme technical sections. Characterized by very rough, rooty, slippery, or rocky sections

gravity check *n.* a fall

hamburger *n.* the condition of skin when geological contact was made with sharp rocks

honk *v.* to vomit due to cycling exertion

impedimentia *n.* all the junk on a bike that impedes performance *and* looks bad

John boy'ed *v.* when a rider's face gets covered with spots of mud, making him look like "John Boy" on the Waltons. "I hit that mudhole and got John boy'ed big time"

kack *n.* an injury to the shin received while doing trials, a kack can be the result of any injury received during technical riding

mud-ectomy 1) *n.* a shower after a ride on a muddy trail 2) *v.* the act of becoming clean

nosepickium *n.* the crusties you pick from your nose after a ride in a dusty environment

Pirelliology *n.* the noble art of being able to identify tires from the tracks they leave on the ground

potato chip *n.* a wheel that has been badly bent

retro-grouch *n.* a rider who prefers an old bike with old components and isn't fond of new, high-tech equipment

Ride On! *n.* a parting phrase used by riders without much else to say

rock-ectomy *v.* removing rocks, dirt, gravel from one's person

tea party *n.* when a whole group of riders stops and chats, and nobody seems to want to ride on

tombstone *n.* one of those little rocks protruding out of the trail that you don't notice because you are having a heart attack climbing the hill

trail mix *n.* the involuntary release of last night's dinner by the way it came in

unobtanium *adj.* describing a bike or accessory made from expensive, high-tech material. A play on "unobtainable" and "titanium"

void *n.* 1) to empty the contents of one's bladder 2) a deep chasm that you have to clear or you will die

whoop-de-doos *n.* a series of up-and-down bumps, suitable for jumping

wild pigs *n.* poorly adjusted brake pads that squeal in use

winky *n.* a reflector

The Zone *n.* a state of mind experienced while riding. You don't think, you just do

Australian cant

The following is a list of underworld vocabulary used by white convicts in Australia in the early 1800s. Many of the terms hailed originally from English prisons.

Bash–to beat
Blow the gaff–to reveal a secret
Bounce–to bully
Cheese it!–stop it!
Dollop–a large quantity of anything
Kid–to deceive
Mizzle–to run away
Office–a hint or signal
School–a number of persons met together to gamble
Up the spout–in pawn

The following words, on the other hand, are often thought of as being English, but were first recorded in Australia.

Word	Australian date	English date
Bike	1869	1890
Chance it	1835	1933
Chain gang	1840	1858
Down under	1900	1908
Paralytic (drunk)	1890	1910
Yum yum	1883	1904

After the First World War words ending with the -o suffix became increasingly popular in Australia. The suffix was often tacked on to place names, and to certain lines of businesses, as in the following list:

Afto–afternoon
Beddo–bed
Bombo–cheap wine
Bottle-o–a bottle collector
Botto–bottle
Bronzo–the anus
Bullo–nonsense
Cacko–very drunk
Cazo–a war casualty
Cobbo–a friend or companion
Confo–conference
Commo–a communist
Compo–worker's compensation
Demo–demonstration
Evo–evening
Garbo–a garbage collector
Jello–jealous
Journo–journalist
Lavo–lavatory
Oppo–opportunity

Pendo–appendix
Prego–pregnant
Salvo–member of the Salvation Army
Sango–sandwich
Spello–rest or break in work

And here are some of the more colorful Australian metaphors:
Buzz around like a blue-arsed fly
Like a duck in a ploughed paddock
Cold enough to freeze the balls of a billiard table
Mopey as a wet hen
Dull as a month of Sundays
So poor he's licking paint off the fence
As free from sense as a frog from feathers
Weaker than a sunburned snowflake

Source: The Australian Language, *Sidney J. Baker, first published 1945*

Australian drinking terms

Slang terms for drunks
Beer swipers
Booze artists
Booze hounds
Booze kings
Boozicians
Boozingtons
Caterpillars
Leanaways
Slurks
Tids
Swippingtons
Jobs
Lolly legs
Shicks

A person who is drunk is said to be:
Blithered
Plonked up
Rotten
Molo
Molly
Stinko
Full as a bull's bum
Half-rinsed
Half-cut
Snockered
Inked
Inkypoo
Pinko
In the grip of the grape

Slang used in the sixties for drinking and drinking bouts
Session
Rort
Beer-up
Booze-up
Break-out
Drunk-up
Grog-up
Jamberoo
Jollo
Perisher
Shivoo
Shiveroo
To go on the scoot
To tip the little finger

Anti–Iraq war slogans

The following is a list of slogans used on the 2003 British marches against the Iraq war.

> Fighting for peace is like screwing for chastity.
> Stop mad cowboy disease.
> Smart bombs don't justify dumb leaders.
> War is so twentieth century.
> Don't mess with Mesopotamia.
> Lets try pre-emptive peace.
> All humanity is downwind.
> Lies, damned lies, and dodgy dossiers.
> Read between the pipelines.
> How did our oil get under their sand?

Things you can't help saying, yet know are really annoying . . .

Fans of the BBC Lancashire Web site compiled a list of really annoying things that despite best intentions they still find themselves saying.

1. You know what I mean?

2. At the end of the day . . .

3. Like

4. I'm not being horrible, but . . .

5. It'll all come out in the wash

6. Whatever

7. If I were you . . .

8. I'll tell you what

9. Ooh . . . er . . . missus

10. Thingy, wotsit

11. I wouldn't do that if you paid me

12. This, that, and the other

13. Etc.

14. So on and so forth

15. Absolutely

16. Erm

17. I won't tell you again, listen

Source: Skiver's Corner, *a feature of the BBC Lancashire Web site,*
www.bbc.co.uk/lancashire/fun

Famous last words

From those scared to go, to those who couldn't wait, here's a list of what the famous reportedly said in their last breath:

This is the last of earth! I am content.
    JOHN QUINCY ADAMS, U.S. President, d. February 23, 1848

Is it not meningitis?
    LOUISA M. ALCOTT, writer, d. March 6, 1888

Waiting are they? Waiting are they? Well—let 'em wait.
In response to an attending doctor who attempted to comfort him

by saying, "General, I fear the angels are waiting for you."
    ETHAN ALLEN, American Revolutionary general, d. February 12, 1789

Am I dying or is this my birthday?
When she woke briefly during her last illness and found all her family around her bedside.
    LADY NANCY ASTOR, d. May 2, 1964

Nothing, but death.
When asked by her sister,
Cassandra, if there was anything
she wanted.
JANE AUSTEN, writer, d. July 18,
1817

*How were the receipts today at
Madison Square Garden?*
P. T. BARNUM, entrepreneur,
d. April 7, 1891

I can't sleep.
JAMES M. BARRIE, author,
d. June 19, 1937

*Is everybody happy? I want
everybody to be happy. I know
I'm happy.*
ETHEL BARRYMORE, actress,
d. June 18, 1959

Now comes the mystery.
HENRY WARD BEECHER, evangelist,
d. March 8, 1887

*Friends applaud, the comedy is
finished.*
LUDWIG VAN BEETHOVEN,
composer, d. March 26, 1827

*I should never have switched from
Scotch to martinis.*
HUMPHREY BOGART, actor,
d. January 14, 1957

Ay Jesus.
CHARLES V, King of France, d. 1380

*I am about to–or I am going to–die:
either expression is correct.*
DOMINIQUE BOUHOURS, French
grammarian, d. 1702

Beautiful.
In reply to her husband who had
asked how she felt.
ELIZABETH BARRETT BROWNING,
writer, d. June 29, 1861

I am still alive!
Stabbed to death by his own
guards (as reported by Roman
historian Tacitus).
GAIUS CALIGULA, Roman
emperor, d. 41 AD

I'm bored with it all.
Before slipping into a coma.
He died nine days later.
WINSTON CHURCHILL, statesman,
d. January 24, 1965

*Damn it . . . Don't you dare ask God
to help me.*
To her housekeeper, who had
begun to pray out loud.
JOAN CRAWFORD, actress,
d. May 10, 1977

My God. What's happened?
DIANA (SPENCER), Princess of
Wales, d. August 31, 1997

I must go in, the fog is rising.
EMILY DICKINSON, poet,
d. May 15, 1886

Please know that I am quite aware
of the hazards. Women must try
to do things as men have tried.
When they fail, their failure must
be but a challenge to others.
Last letter to her husband before
her last flight.
KHAQQ calling Itasca. We must be
on you, but cannot see you.
Gas is running low.
Last radio communiqué before
her disappearance.
AMELIA EARHART,
disappeared July 2, 1937

All my possessions
for a moment of time.
ELIZABETH I, Queen of England,
d. 1603

I've never felt better.
DOUGLAS FAIRBANKS, SR., actor,
d. December 12, 1939

Turn up the lights, I don't want to
go home in the dark.
O. HENRY (WILLIAM SIDNEY
PORTER), writer, d. June 5, 1910

I see black light.
VICTOR HUGO, writer,
d. May 22, 1885

Let's cool it, brothers . . .
Spoken to his assassins, three men
who shot him fifteen times.
MALCOLM X, Black leader,
d. February 21, 1965

Go on, get out–last words are for
fools who haven't said enough.
To his housekeeper, who urged
him to tell her his last words so
she could write them down for
posterity.
KARL MARX, revolutionary,
d. March 14, 1883

Nothing matters. Nothing matters.
LOUIS B. MAYER, film producer,
d. October 29, 1957

It's all been very interesting.
LADY MARY WORTLEY MONTAGU,
writer, d. August 21, 1762

I knew it. I knew it. Born in a hotel
room–and Goddamn it–died in a
hotel room.
EUGENE O'NEILL, writer,
d. November 27, 1953

I've had eighteen straight whiskies,
I think that's the record . . .
DYLAN THOMAS, poet,
d. November 9, 1953

Get my swan costume ready.
ANNA PAVLOVA, ballerina,
d. January 23, 1931

I love you, Sarah. For all eternity,
I love you.
Spoken to his wife.
JAMES K. POLK, U.S. President,
d. 1849

I owe much; I have nothing; the rest
I leave to the poor.
FRANÇOIS RABELAIS, writer, d. 1553

They couldn't hit an elephant at
this dist . . .
Killed in battle during
U.S. Civil War.
GENERAL JOHN SEDGWICK, Union
commander, d. 1864

Woe is me. Methinks I'm turning
into a god.
VESPASIAN, Roman emperor,
d. 79 AD

Go away. I'm all right.
H. G. WELLS, novelist,
d. August 13, 1946

Either that wallpaper goes, or I do.
OSCAR WILDE, writer,
d. November 30, 1900

Source: www.corsinet.com

Epitaphs

Some epitaphs, taken from gravestones in the United States and the UK, are worth remembering for their wit or wisdom, even though the people concerned might be long forgotten.

On the grave of Ezekial Aikle in
East Dalhousie Cemetery, Nova Scotia
Here lies
Ezekial Aikle
Age 102
The Good
Die Young.

In a cemetery in London, England
Here lies Ann Mann,
Who lived an old maid
But died an old Mann.
Dec. 8, 1767

In a Ruidoso, New Mexico, cemetery
Here lies
Johnny Yeast
Pardon me
For not rising.

In a Silver City, Nevada, cemetery
Here lays Butch,
We planted him raw.
He was quick on the trigger,
But slow on the draw.

A lawyer's epitaph in England
Sir John Strange
Here lies an honest lawyer,
And that is Strange.

Someone determined to be
anonymous in Stowe, Vermont
I was somebody.
Who, is no business
Of yours.

A widow wrote this epitaph in a Vermont cemetery
Sacred to the memory of
my husband John Barnes
who died January 3, 1803.
His comely young widow, aged 23, has
many qualifications of a good wife, and
yearns to be comforted.

In a Georgia cemetery

I told you I was sick!

In a cemetery in Hartscombe, England

On the 22nd of June
Jonathan Fiddle–
Went out of tune.

Someone in Winslow, Maine didn't like Mr. Wood

In Memory of Beza Wood
Departed this life
Nov. 2, 1837
Aged 45 yrs.
Here lies one Wood
Enclosed in wood
One Wood
Within another.
The outer wood
Is very good:
We cannot praise
The other.

Owen Moore in Battersea, London, England

Gone away
Owin' more
Than he could pay.

On a grave from the 1880s in Nantucket, Massachusetts

Under the sod and under the trees
Lies the body of Jonathan Pease.
He is not here, there's only the pod:
Pease shelled out and went to God.

The grave of Ellen Shannon in Girard, Pennsylvania
Who was fatally burned
March 21, 1870
by the explosion of a lamp
filled with "R. E. Danforth's
Non-Explosive Burning Fluid"

In a Thurmont, Maryland, cemetery
Here lies an Atheist
All dressed up
And no place to go.

Dr. Fred Roberts, Brookland, Arkansas
Office upstairs.

In Newbury, England (1742)
Tom Smith is dead, and here he lies,
Nobody laughs and nobody cries;
Where his soul's gone, or how it fares,
Nobody knows, and nobody cares.

The Tired Woman's Epitaph
Here lies a poor woman who was always tired;
She lived in a house where help was not hired.
Her last words on earth were: "Dear friends, I am going
Where washing ain't done, nor sweeping, nor sewing:
But everything there is exact to my wishes;
For where they don't eat there's no washing of dishes . . .
Don't mourn for me now; don't mourn for me never—
I'm going to do nothing for ever and ever."

To the Memory of Abraham Beaulieu
Born 15 September 1822
Accidentally shot
4th April 1844
As a mark of affection
from his brother.

On an innkeeper (1875)
0eneath this stone, in hopes of Zion,
Doth lie the landlord of the Lion;
His son keeps on the business still,
Resigned unto the heavenly will.

Source: www.blakjak.demon.co.uk

The first printed
shopping list

Online museum of
shopping lists

Too lazy
to make lists?

A list of 10 things to do
after reading this book

LISTS
ABOUT
LISTS

Finally, for those interested in lists, just as lists, the art of, the collection of, not really for their content, just for their very wonderful existence, here are three interesting lists.

The first printed shopping list

There's no proof of this, but we like to think that in the first edition of this book, back in 1980, we printed what could well have been the first shopping list to appear in a nonfiction book–in novels they had been used long before that–and revealed the existence of the first known collector of shopping lists. OK, the first we had ever known about. A Mrs. Louise Gill from Devon wrote to tell us how it all began.

Exeter, Devon, 20 January 1980.

Dear Mr. Davies,

In my college days I began a scrapbook of lists, collected on pavements, in library books, and on supermarket floors. These lists were mostly shopping lists, probably the lists most often written in everyday life, especially by women. This collection consisted of lists written on various articles, from old Christmas cards to torn-out diary pages. I now have a collection of sixty shopping lists in my scrapbook.

This is the very first list I acquired, found on a café table complete with the biro, in the summer of 1974 at the Princess Pavilion, Falmouth, Cornwall–now called the Tivoli Biergarten. It is certainly an odd mixture of items!

½ yd orange velvet velcro (green or lilac)
12 lemon squeezers
Body Language bra 36A
Dress
My necklace
Prescription
Bar of Old English Lavender soap
Records
Mincemeat

Online museum of shopping lists

Ever wondered what happened to the shopping list you scribbled on an old envelope last week and which has since disappeared? One answer could be it was picked up from the supermarket floor, scanned, and sent to the world's first Online Museum of Shopping Lists.

The Web site is for everyone who is curious about what other people shop for, and those who believe the shopping list is a dying art. To the Web site owners, the shopping list "represents a symbol of our vanishing individuality as we grow daily more uniform, passive, and accepting." While you can easily discover what people have bought by studying their cash-register receipts, "the list they have written before going out to the shops tells you about what they want and what they think they might need."

Among the online shopping list exhibits are:
Bleach
White trash-can liners
Black bags
Dog collar
Ariel liquid
Bubble bath
Shower gel–pink
Car
Clothes pegs
Mouthwash
Radio-controlled car

Things we need for the house (all as written)
Pine Soul
Papper towels
Toilet papper
Detergent liquet
Dishwash liquet
Forbreeze
Shampoo/conditioner

Soup
Pads (for me)
Get money order for $23.14
One Electric bill
$8.00 birth certificate

Too lazy to make lists?

There is also a Web site, www.lifesaverlists, that will help you compile lists, if you are too tired, too bored, or too listless to bother doing your own. They have an array of ready-made lists, on a variety of topics, to help you, for example, when you're about to go out shopping. The site also promises to act as "your personal organizer" for small daily tasks, holiday planning, or big celebrations. The Web site even offers tips about how to look after our lists, so that you can use them again. Well, you wouldn't want to muck them up, would you?

Their top list tip is as follows: "After printing out your list, place it in a plastic sleeve and use a dry-erase marker to check off items from the list as necessary. When finished using your list, simply wipe the sleeve clean with a tissue and the list is instantly reusable!"

We put in two topics, just to see what sort of stuff they would list for us, one on pampered pets and the other on what to put in your gym bag.

The pampered pet
Everything your pampered pet needs:
Toenail clippers (keep them sharp)
Sharp scissors (trimming fur from pads of feet)
Quality shampoo for dogs (for color and nondrying for skin)
Toothbrush and toothpaste
Leash and collar
Chew toy (so they don't chew your toys)
Nutritious snacks or "treats"
Brushes and combs (brush for coat/comb for skin)
"Splat mat" for under the food and water bowls

What to put in your gym bag
Towel and facecloth
Large bath towel
Body sponge
Deodorant
Baby powder
Body and facial cleansers
Moisturizers (face and body)
Shampoo and conditioner
Brush and comb
Flip-flops for in the shower
Hair dryer
Cosmetics
Bathing suit
Swimming goggles
Nose plugs
Extra T-shirt
Extra sweatshirt
Extra socks
Extra sweatpants
Shorts
Bottled water
Energy bar
Sweatbands

A list of 10 things to do after reading this book

1. Pay for it. Especially if you have been standing for two hours in a bookshop reading it. You mean thing. Publishers and booksellers have to live.

2. Get it out again. That's if you have borrowed it from the library. There is a system called PLR–Public Lending Right–whereby authors get a small amount of money based on a random sample of library borrowings. Authors, too, have a right to live.

3. Tell all your friends how excellent, amusing, and informative it was.

4. Even if you haven't quite finished. Or even got halfway.

5. Buy several copies. You can already tell it will make a first-class birthday, Christmas, special present for all ages, all types, so why not get it now, before you forget.

6. Don't write in with any spelling mistakes, literals, or other mistakes you have spotted. Boring, boring.

7. If, of course, there are any, which is highly unlikely.

8. Anyway, we're bound to have caught them by now.

9. But do write in if you have any favorite lists, of any sort, which you have created or spotted somewhere. If we use them in the next edition of the book, your name will be credited and a uniformed messenger, i.e. postman, will deliver a free copy of the book to your door.

10. Hmm, that's it. Thanks for reading.